Politics and Society in Scottish Thought

Edited and Introduced
by Shinichi Nagao

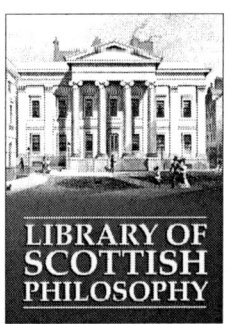

IMPRINT ACADEMIC

Copyright © Shinichi Nagao, 2007

The moral rights of the author have been asserted.
No part of any contribution may be reproduced in any form
without permission, except for the quotation of brief passages
in criticism and discussion.

Published in the UK by Imprint Academic
PO Box 200, Exeter EX5 5HY, UK

Published in the USA by Imprint Academic
Philosophy Documentation Center
PO Box 7147, Charlottesville, VA 22906-7147, USA

ISBN 978 0907845 782

A CIP catalogue record for this book is available from the
British Library and US Library of Congress

Full series details:

www.imprint-academic.com/losp

Contents

    Series Editor's Note iv

    Introduction 1

I. The Discovery of Modern Market Society

    1. David Hume (1711–1776)
        Of the Original Contract (1748) 29
        Of Refinement in the Arts (1752) 43
    2. Adam Smith (1723–1790)
        Lectures on Jurisprudence (1766) 53

II. Governing the Market

    3. James Steuart (1712–1780)
        An Inquiry into the Principles
        of Political Economy (1767) 83
    4. Adam Ferguson (1723–1816)
        An Essay on the History of Civil Society (1767) . . 107

III. Utopian Imagination and Radical Reforms

    5. Robert Wallace (1697–1771)
        Various Prospects on Mankind, Nature
        and Providence (1761) 133
    6. William Ogilvie (1736–1819)
        An Essay on the Right of Property
        in Land (1782) 162
    7. Thomas Reid (1710–1796)
        Some Thoughts on the Utopian System (1794) . . . 179

    Bibliography 201

    Index 203

Series Editor's Note

The principal purpose of volumes in this series is not to provide scholars with accurate editions, but to make the writings of Scottish philosophers accessible to a new generation of modern readers in an attractively produced and competitively priced format. In accordance with this purpose, certain changes have been made to the original texts:

- Spelling and punctuation have been modernized.
- In some cases, the selected passages have been given new titles.
- Some original footnotes and references have not been included.
- Some extracts have been shortened from their original length.
- Quotations from Greek have been transliterated, and passages in foreign languages translated, or omitted altogether.

Care has been taken to ensure that in no instance do these amendments truncate the argument or alter the meaning intended by the original author. For readers who want to consult the original texts, full bibliographical details are provided for each extract.

The Library of Scottish Philosophy was originally an initiative of the Centre for the Study of Scottish Philosophy at the University of Aberdeen. The first six volumes, published in 2004, were commissioned with financial support from the Carnegie Trust for the Universities of Scotland, and the texts prepared for publication by Mr Jon Cameron, administrative and editorial assistant to the Centre. In 2006 the CSSP moved to Princeton where it became one of three research centers within the Special Collections of Princeton Theological Seminary. The next four volumes were prepared for publication by the new administrative and editorial assistant, Ms Elaine James.

Acknowledgements

The CSSP gratefully acknowledges the support of the Carnegie Trust, the first class work of both Mr Cameron and Ms James, the enthusiasm and excellent service of the publisher Imprint Academic, and the permission of the University of Aberdeen Special Collections and Libraries to use the engraving of the *Faculty of Advocates* (1829) as the logo for the series.

Gordon Graham,
Princeton, May 2007

Introduction

The title of the present volume could be misleading. The volume will not give a compact picture of the political and social thought that has been developed in Scotland. Instead, it will furnish readers with a prospect of it, that is, the way the political and social philosophers of 18th century Scotland tried to answer the following question: What is, and what ought to be, the relationship between the modern market and stable, desirable social order? The essays collected here belong to the second half of the century and will give only a snapshot of the entire achievements of the Scots on political and social philosophy.

The editor of the volume believes that he has good reasons to approach the subject in this way. As the editor's name suggests, the major works of Scottish political and social philosophers in the 18th century have been read and studied throughout the world. The significance of the Scottish contribution on the issue transcends British or European contexts. For example, after *The Wealth of Nations,* the masterpiece of Scottish Enlightenment in the genre, appeared in European languages, it was translated into Japanese at the end of 19th century and into Chinese at the beginning of the 20th century. The various translations of the book itself show the variety of cultural and historical contexts in which the projects were done, and consequently its universal appeal.[1]

The Scottish Enlightenment is known as the birth place of modern social sciences. It is true that it tried to solve the problems arising from modern market economy typically exemplified in neighboring England. But its universal and undying humanist

---

[1] In Japan, it was translated into a modern Japanese that was the product of the country's modernisation that began in the middle of the 19th century. In China, Yen Fu, himself an important modernizer, replaced Smith's 18th century English in his edition with classical Chinese that is hard for modern Chinese students to read.

appeal is not confined to the fact that it gave birth to the liberal market theory. Its interests and concerns were rather political and sociological. Scottish moral philosophers discussed, gave lectures and wrote, in attempts to give answer to the question of how to harmonize a modern market economy with ethics, social order, stable polity and the moral progress of human race. Philosophers felt that there was no automatic mechanism between them and therefore some political and sociological devices were needed. Recent scholarship has successfully demonstrated that Adam Smith was neither a lasses-faire economist nor an outright liberal democrat. As his lectures on jurisprudence will tell, he had complicated views on the consequences of a modern market economy. His "economics" was a part of his comprehensive political theory in which landlords and labourers had their own roles with mercantile classes.

Furthermore, Scottish philosophers' prescription was not univocal. They sometimes fell into contradiction with each other. The recommendations range over the numbers of policies from liberal polity to the complete abolition of private property. As a collective entity, Scots failed to find one clear cut solution. The very diversity of their conclusions, together with the thoroughness and sincerity of their endeavours, make the works of Scottish philosophers relevant to peoples' lives in every part of the world in the age of globalization. The task of this introduction is to highlight the concerns that guided their thinking, the variety of answers they gave to the public, and the uniqueness of their views that is now sometimes forgotten.

Common Agenda

The establishment of economics and social sciences are not solely the invention of some Scottish independent genius, but rather the result of a collective effort to solve the puzzles discussed in a homogeneous intellectual community that existed in the form of clubs and societies. The community was well-placed for the task. It was located within the boundary of British Empire so that philosophers could observe and experience the most rapidly developing market economy of the age. They were able to look at it from the outside as well, for, with its own laws, universities, national church and social relations, Scots still had a degree of independence from England. While the Scottish intellectual community was able to maintain an appropriate distance from the centre of the commercial empire, it also had its own network with the continent, mostly with Netherlands and France. This gave Scottish philosophers a milieu that enabled them to think in cosmopolitan ways and to belong to the republic of letters, rather than becoming the citizens of the empire. The way they considered the socio-politico-economic questions of the age was, therefore, both practical and philosophical, British and European, or European and universal. These characteristics of Scottish endeavours endowed their works with a unique referential value, even for today's readers.

The following list of "questions" discussed in the Select Society of Edinburgh will give a hint to the framework within which major works of the Scottish Enlightenment took shape. The society was the parliament of the intellectual community of the country. Most of the authors of this volume took part in it and other similar societies. Adam Smith, Adam Ferguson and Robert Wallace were the members of the Select Society. Smith and Ferguson presided over its meetings. Hume took the secretarial responsibilities of several important societies including the Philosophical Society of Edinburgh, which became the Royal Society at the end of the century. Thomas Reid had his own societies such as the Philosophical Society of Aberdeen when he was in King's College and the Literary Society of Glasgow while he worked as the professor of moral philosophy of Glasgow University. The meetings of a society usually consisted of two parts, reading and discussing essays written by its members and making arguments on a question. Questions to be discussed next time were announced at the end of the meeting. The following questions concerning political and social matters were frequently on agenda at other societies and clubs, too.

1. Does the increase of trade and manufacture naturally promote the happiness of a nation?
2. Whether is a nation on a state of barbarity, or a nation of luxury and refined manners the happiest.
3. Whether doth landed or a commercial interest contribute most to the tranquility and stability of a state.
4. Whether luxury be advantageous to any state.

5. Whether a nation once sunk in luxury and pleasure can be retrieved and brought back to any degree of worth and excellence.
6. Whether in the ancient times of every nation the people were not stronger, of body healthier, and longer lived than in late times.[2]

It is obvious that the issue of the emergence of a modern market economy was placed in a much broader context in the discussions at these societies than the matters of pure economics, that is how to manage the market. The issue was one of the central themes of political science because it was thought that economic growth tended to threaten social order and political stability based upon the active participation of citizens. It was a cultural problem as well and treated in the fashionable framework of the century, of the comparison between the ancient and the modern. It was seen as a matter of psychology and ethics as well as of political economy. It was related to the prospects of the ethical advancement of human race. The focal point is, whether it is possible that a modern market economy driven by the self-interest of humans can become compatible with the order and stability of society and with the dignity and moral progress of mankind; and if so, how and when this coexistence will be achieved.

New Science of a Society

It is not easy to find a plausible explanation as to why such a small country ever could be a cradle of many great achievements of the Enlightenment, especially in the disciplines we now call "social sciences". There could be several possible reasons: There was an active social life in Scottish cities, of clubs and societies, as we have seen, and an homogeneous, well-educated social elite who lost the political control of their country to Westminster. They could only do something related to the social and cultural issues of their home land. But the early introduction of "new science" into the Scottish educational system and the intellectual life of its social elite must have contributed significantly to the emergence of social sciences in the country too.

University reform and the introduction of "new science", especially of Newtonianism, are the remarkable features of the Scot-

[2] *Minutes of the Procedure of the Select Society*, National Library of Scotland, MS 23.1.1.

tish educational system in the first half of the century. As a result, the country had advanced educational institutions and the prevailing scientific mindset, which examined matters of nature, morality, politics and religion with the same epistemological and methodological point of view. "Experimental philosophy", thought by intellectuals to have been successfully exemplified by Isaac Newton and John Locke at the beginning of the century, was the buzz word of the century. Consequently, it was very natural to think that philosophers' task was to succeed the project launched by Locke and to establish the science of humans and society with Newton's methodology, as well as to continue the intellectual conquest of nature in chemistry, medicine, geology, electricity and magnetism with tools invented by him. The works of Hume, Smith, Ferguson and other figures in socio-political philosophy were the products of the same collective endeavour that directed the scientific researches of Colin MacLaurin, William Cullen, Joseph Black and James Hutton.

However, the ways they carried out the tasks were significantly different. Many held the orthodox Newtonian view of the Royal Society of London in which moderate Christian beliefs coexisted with the latest discovery of natural science in the form of natural theology. Realist attitudes toward ethical matters were predominant among them. Hume did not share this configuration of ideas and was very critical of the majority's view. Smith took a different position in ethics, too. In methodology and epistemology, all these Scots were seemingly Newtonian, or at least the supporters of the term "experimental philosophy". Their positions and techniques, however, differed substantially. Let's take the example of Smith again.

Although the economic theory of Adam Smith has been often characterized as an adaptation of Newtonianism in the social sciences, his interpretation of Newtonian method was very peculiar. He once characterized the Newtonian method in *The Lectures on Rhetoric and Belles Lettres* as to "lay down certain principles known or proved in the beginning, from whence we account for the several Phenomena, connecting all together by the same Chain." Furthermore, he stated that "Des-Cartes was in reality the first who attempted this method." Smith made a two-fold mistake in this explanation. Firstly, Descartes was the target at which Newton's criticism aimed in *Principia*. There are numerous attacks on Cartesian philosophy in the writings of British Newtonians and most of them accused him of employing a false method in empirical sciences, the very method that Smith called Newtonian in the lectures, that is, the method of deductive reasoning. Therefore, Newtonian method and Cartesian method are not at all identical as Smith explained above. Secondly, the method Smith described should be called Aristotelian method, the method of individual sciences described in the *Posterior Analytics*, instead of Newtonian method. The methodology employed in *The Wealth of Nations* has no resemblance to that of Newtonian science, except for the fact that Smith consciously constructed his system deductively from the first and self-evident principle, such as the propensity to exchange or the function of sympathy. It looks as if Smith had followed Newton in the first two of "the rules of philosophizing" of the *Principia*, the parsimonious principles that require that axiomatic principles should be few in number, but not in the second two, the need for experimental proofs in theoretical reasoning.

However, the empiricist aspect of Smith's method cannot be overlooked. Natural history was another source of the influence that natural sciences had on 18th century social sciences, especially Scottish social sciences including Smith's works. Smith's methodology is a hybrid of Aristotelian method and the method of natural history in the following way: instead of demonstrating theorems from axiomatic propositions, natural history collects data and classifies them. For Smith, this method is supplementary to his deductive reasoning because he presupposed certain principles to be true, such as sympathy and natural price, before the inductive processes begin. Thus allowing the universality of the results of deductive reasoning from supposed general principles, natural history serves his theories as the explanatory tool to justify the deviations of existing systems from general laws, finding particular conditions derived from geographical, historical and situational contingencies.

Though not exactly a product of a rigorous empiricist version of Newtonian methodology, the Smithian system of social sciences was a byproduct of the developments of the 18th century sciences. Smith was not an inventor of a "system", the "fabricated" knowledge system of the universe, as the doctrines of Descartes or Leibnitz were thought to be in 18th century Britain. Smith was one of the "empirical scientists" of 18th century Scotland, who claimed to have found the principles of sub-systems, of chemical processes, of market economy, of the human body, which were essential parts of the entire world created by God. This aspect of Smith's scientific projects is, if not exactly Newtonian, still very characteristically Scottish, in the sense that Scottish scientists in that century, started from Newtonian aspirations and methodological formats, and bravely endeavored to carry out premature attempts to build the self-sufficient explanatory bodies of knowledge. In so doing, they stood out among their contemporaries in Britain as the imaginative theorists of 18th century sciences, as S. Mason wrote in his *A History of Sciences*.[3]

Self-interest and State

The rest of this chapter will treat each essay in this volume. They run from the discovery of a market society at the beginning to its abolition at the end. David Hume is the first author in this perspective. Hume is the most important philosopher of the Scottish Enlightenment. Today he is regarded as a prominent economist, social theorist, as well as one of the discoverers of a modern market society. The ascendance of David Hume toward the pantheon of philosophy and social sciences had been so impressive that we tend to forget that he was standing on the fringe of the intellectual landscape of the Scottish Enlightenment. Hume was the greatest skeptic of the age in his country. Everybody enjoyed the game of criticizing him. Eventually, his skeptical arguments became the catalyst of Enlightenment thought. Scottish philosophy was born as the result of the efforts to construct effective counter arguments against Hume's philosophy.

Hume's contribution to social theory was profound. In the essay "Of original contract", he effectively demolished social contract theory that was one of the basis of Whigish political theory. This philosophical attack on the ideological foundation of the Glorious Revolution was interpreted as being originated in his conservative political attitude by radical Lockians like Reid. But by doing so, he opened up the scope to the empirical research into the origins of society and authority. In philosophical contexts, Hume formally expressed his intentions to follow the method of John Locke, and then dramatically destroyed his master's philosophy in his first and major philosophical work, *A Treatise on Human Nature*. He continued this destructive-constructive restructuring

---

[3] S.F. Mason, *A History of Sciences* (London: Routledge and Kegan Paul, 1953), Chapter 24.

of British empiricism in his treatises on politics and society and became a founder of modern socio-political theory and ethics. In initiating the conceptual change of the reference points from contract to utility, from natural jurisprudence to convention, he succeeded in separating the principles of social order from ethics and virtue. He also found the origin of government not in an original contract but in violence, as V.I. Lenin did in *The State and Revolution*.

Hume was a forerunner of the classical school of political economy, too. Although Hume, as an economic theorist, could not believe in the endless progress of nations in terms of economic development, his essays on money, trade and population are the precursors to those of Steuart and Smith. He favoured liberal economic policy and made arguments against Mercantilist theory and policies so persuasively that he set the cornerstone for the further development of economics. However, he was not an "economist" in today's sense. His essays on political economy were always accompanied by the sociological point of view. The "interdisciplinarity" of his observations enabled him to grasp the role of "luxury" in a modern market society. On the one hand, it creates "effective demand" in Keynesian sense, and ignites and maintains economic growth. On the other hand, the diffusion of luxury to the members of a market society brings sophistication of taste and deepened interdependence, thus strengthening social bonds that could replace "public virtue" in ancient polity. Discovering the economics and sociology of a consumer society, Hume refuted his opponents' proposition that the self-interest axiom of actors in a market society would destroy that society. Hume was able to find the origin of the stability and order of a market society in its very nature. Eventually Hume came to represent modernity in the political and social philosophy of his century.

But it is not correct to try to say that Hume was a forefather of liberalism in the 19th and 20th centuries. As a skeptic, he acknowledged well the serious defects of a modern market society. He predicted that British monetary empire would corrupt soon because of huge public debts. He did not approve the continuity of economic success of wealthy nations and favoured the view of their cyclical downfall. He did not believe in the economic and political supremacy of liberal democracy over other forms of government. On the whole, Hume was a skeptic philosopher who was able to support a modern market society and still remained very critical of it.

The ambivalence toward modern market society can be seen even in the works of Adam Smith, the discoverer of a modern market society and the founder of economics and economic liberalism. Smith, a young friend of Hume, synthesized the theory of a modern market society in his "system of natural liberty". Smith emerged as such in his lectures on moral philosophy at Glasgow University. Francis Hutcheson, Smith's teacher at the university, had already taught him the major issues of political economy, such as labour, price and money, though not systematically. There are many other works from which Smith learned. If we adopt J.A. Schumpeter's cynical view, the genius of Smith was in the very ability to put many arguments previously made by other writers together in a beautiful and seamless narrative with the help of few guiding principles, namely self-interest, the propensity to exchange, and the division of labour. But even if Schumpeter is absolutely right, it is still certainly an achievement to complete and publish *The Wealth of Nations*. The theoretical parts of the book, except those apparently influenced by Francois Quesnay, were already presented to students in his lectures at Glasgow University.

As with every figure in the history of philosophy's hall of fame, there are many misconceptions of Adam Smith's views caused by the simplification of his doctrines made in succeeding centuries. He was not an enthusiast of liberal market fundamentalism. He never forgot to mention that the division of labour had the tendency to make a person unable to become a responsible citizen. He supported the roles of the state in protecting its citizens from external and internal insecurity, educating them properly and investing in public goods that could not be financed by private sectors. Taxation was therefore not a necessary evil but a "necessary good" for him. It is very likely that he thought that governing a country was the responsibility of its natural rulers, of a landlord class, though he emphasized the importance of individuals' initiatives and taught statesmen in his books not to ignore the knowledge and motivations of ordinary people. He did not trust mercantile classes because he anticipated that their interests tended to be against public interest, often ended up in the mistreatments of labourers, the formation of monopoly and the corruptions of government, therefore the competition among them must necessarily be introduced against their wills by the ruling class of a country. No phrase like "cheap government", "tax burden", "deregulation", or "liberal democracy" can be found in his writings. These ideas were the fabrications of later followers of Smith who rarely read the whole of *The Wealth of Nations*.

It is worth mentioning that his theory of political economy forms the second chapter of his theory of politics. This part treats the internal policies of a country, its "police". The aim of "police" is to bring peace and happiness to citizens. Smith stressed at the beginning of this part of his lectures that the prosperity of a nation creates the stability and order of its polity. For him, economic growth is not the end of "police", but the most effective means to achieve the goals of internal policies. One of the unique facets of his political economy is that he made it independent from the form of government and other topics of politics. Adam Ferguson, the professor of moral philosophy of Edinburgh University, treated political economy in relation to the matter of national defense. Alexander Gerard, in his lectures on moral philosophy at Aberdeen, discussed what kind of government was most fitted to promote economic growth. For Smith, with his friend David Hume, the policies of "the natural system of liberty" could be adapted by several forms of government. They supposed that it was able to be implemented in France under the rule of absolute monarchy. If interpreted correctly, Smith's views on "economic liberalism" were perfectly in harmony with quasi-democratic one party rule in post-war Japan, the dictatorship for development seen in South Korea, Singapore, Taiwan (etc.), and even with the communist regime in present day China. In short, Smith was not an advocate of North American ideology in the present century. What mattered most to him was not political liberty itself, but the external and internal peace of a country and the material welfare of ordinary citizens, which, in the end, bring the progress of humankind toward moral perfection.

It is also important to notice that there are some contradictive and self-defeating remarks in his writings. He boldly declared that the system of natural liberty was the true system of political economy in the part treating physiocracy of his masterpiece. But in his philosophical essay on the history of astronomy, he explained that every system of philosophy, including Newtonian natural philosophy, was the creation of human psychology and therefore would be replaced by new ones in the future. So be it, then his system of natural liberty must have the same destiny, too. In the third book of *The Wealth of Nations*, he described the natural course of the development of investment from agriculture to foreign trade. Then he argued that the economic history of Europe after the decay of the Roman Empire followed the opposite course, from foreign trade to agriculture, and it was very foolish if one hoped to reverse the development. If he was really a sincere student of experimental philosophy, he could not formulise the theory of "natural course", because it contradicted empirical evidence that he himself supplied in the same book. If he really believed what he theoretically stated, he must have supported physiocrats. Even in his first and a successful publication, *The Theory of Moral Sentiments*, he seems to have been unable to decide between ancient, heroic, stoic virtue and modern morality seen among the "middling ranks" of a modern society.

Maybe his personality issues contributed to these inconsistencies. A lady once described Smith as "ugly like a devil". He had a sort of mental illness that haunted him all his life. Hume happily spent a bachelor's life, but Smith failed twice in his love affairs and never married. He characterized philosophy in "the history of astronomy" as a product of human fear against irregularities and surprise that sometimes, he said, killed a man. Unlike sociable, handsome and lovely David Hume, he hid a dark side of his personality beneath the surface of his perfect narrative as an Enlightenment philosopher.

But it is natural that philosophical reasons are there as well. If so, this is not a dishonour to Smith. This is rather the evidence that Smith was again one of the sincere thinkers of the Scottish Enlightenment who considered the merits and the defects of a modern society, contradictions between wealth, power and the ethical progress of human kind very seriously and very thoroughly. As the result, even though Smith seems to have definitely decided to stand by modernity more than any other philosophers in the country, he still had ambivalence to and reservations about it.

Imbalance and Corruption

While Smith was able to present a plausible explanation for how a modern market system could function well, James Steuart played the role of pointing out the inner defects and malfunctions of it. Some may hesitate to honour Steuart with the title of a "Scottish Enlightenment philosopher". Most of the literati and the scientists of the Enlightenment were religiously moderate or deist, and politically standing for the union, or at least, not against Westminster's rule. Sir James Steuart was born and educated in the country. He joined the Jacobite rebellion in 1745. Consequently he had to leave his country and stayed in the continent. When he was allowed to come back to his homeland, he brought the plan and materials for a splendid gift to Britain. It is the first comprehensive book ever written in English on the "principles of political economy". Although the book was welcomed by the public and intellectuals alike, it became almost forgotten in later years. When J.M. Keynes revived the theory of effective demand against free market policies, he only named T.H. Multhus as his predecessor, despite the fact that the major founder of the theory was actually James Steuart. Certainly his book was widely read in the late 18th century. Even G.W.F. Hegel read it in a German translation and there are traces of Steuart's influence in Hegel's texts. But the person whom it inspired most could be Adam Smith, because it appeared just when he had formulated his ideas on police in his lectures and was about to write his major works. It is tempting to imagine that Smith, astonished by the publication of the *Principles*, changed his publication plan and began to write a book on police, the second part of his lectures, instead of completing the first part of his Jurisprudence, on justice. However, Smith never mentioned Steuart's name in his major work and the success of *the Wealth of Nations* washed away *Principles*.

Steuart's view is pictorially represented in the following metaphor. Smith writes that an artificial intervention will destroy the harmony of an economy driven by the self-interest of citizens:

> It (this bounty) breaks what may be called the natural balance of industry.[4]

Steuart says that a modern state and a society are so developed that they need more careful management than primitive polity: "It is of government as of machines, the more they are simple, the more they are solid and lasting; the more they are artfully composed, the more they become useful; but the more apt they are to be out of order." (James Steuart, *An Inquiry into the Principles of Political Economy*, London, 1777, pp. 249–50.) He goes on to say,

---

[4] Adam Smith, *Lectures on Jurisprudence*, Oxford U.P.,1978, p. 498.

> The Lacedemonian form may be compared to the wedge, the most solid and compact of all the mechanical powers. Those of modern states to watches, which are continually going wrong; sometimes the spring is found too weak, at the other times too strong for the machine: and when the wheels are not made according to a determined proportion, by the able hands of a Graham, or a Julien le Roy, they do not tally well with one another; then the machine stops, and if it be forced, some part gives away; and the workman's hand becomes necessary to set it right.[5]

Steuart was very aware that the driving force of a modern market economy was individuals' initiatives to seek their own interests. His point is that, although the market system is the most efficient in producing material wealth, it sometimes causes imbalance within itself and there is no automatic mechanism that ensures the system will recover from it. His warning comes therefore not from the denial of the reality of a market system, but from the very cognition of the sophistication and the complexity of it. His analysis of money as an economic theorist is also worth mentioning. Smith and the classical school were so obsessed with refuting mercantile writers that they paid little attention to money as an independent variable. Steuart's words sound very meaningful in the age of globalization when most of the population of the human race is forced to live in a polarized global society run by the global circulation of money with frequent economic disturbance and ever-growing anxieties. Where to find the "careful hand of a statesman" to correct the imbalance is the major contemporary political problem. The works of Steuart and Smith thus must be seen as non-identical twins that cannot be separated in the theoretical consideration of a market system.

Although Adam Ferguson's fame has never reached the heights of Hume and Smith, he was one of the most internationally influential social philosophers of the Scottish Enlightenment. Karl Marx praised him for writing the "first history of civil society". Ferguson has regularly been mentioned in the textbooks of the history of sociology as the founder of modern sociology. Now some writers begin to give him the honour of discovering neo-conservative social theory.

However, it is not entirely accurate to characterize him as the representative figure of republicanism and public spirit in the

---

[5] James Steuart, *An Inquiry into the Principles of Political Economy*, London, 1777, pp. 249–50.

Enlightenment. Being fluent both in Gaelic and Latin, he always maintained a historical perspective that often gave him an insight of historical relativism. Being a very active member of Scottish intellectual institutions, such as the church, universities, clubs and societies, he never lost touch with the reality of modern life and fully realized the importance and efficiency of the division of labour and the market that constitute the system of a modern commercial society. The sympathy towards the ancients and republican spirit did not make him an anachronistic admirer of ancient times nor another Jean-Jacques Rousseau, but an impartial observer of both ancient and modern societies.

The perspective of a social scientist never prevented him from becoming a popular teacher of moral philosophy in his university. Science was not yet understood as a value-free cognitive process. He shared the conviction with other Scottish philosophers that the method of experimental philosophy most successfully demonstrated by Newton could ensure the ethical foundation of righteous human conduct as well as unveil the laws that govern nature and society. He tried to discover the foundation of virtue and morality in human nature with the help of the method of natural history. With Steuart, Ferguson's approach in moral philosophy was more empiricist than Hume and Smith. It made him the founder of sociology.

Moreover, he was one of the early social critics of modern market society. As a historian and a sociologist, he understood the principles of modern society in comparison to the ancient. In so doing, he clearly recognized the fact that the division of labour was the origin of wealth in a modern society, that the division of labour presupposed the liberty to have private property and thus liberal polity was most adequate to a modern market society. But he never forgot to point out that the division of labour tended to make people merely the gears of society, rather than active human beings. This insight immediately reminds us of Karl Marx's theory of alienation 100 years later. He also warned that, with the words of Max Weber 150 years later, the establishment of a modern society as a huge machine could end up in the loss of the energy and passion of its citizens. He described two threats that endanger the liberty of a modern society. The one is the enemy from outside. The other is the despotism originating in the passive attitude of citizens. The latter example sounds very prophetic, as if Ferguson had foreseen the emergence of totalitarianism in the 20th century.

An active principle of human behaviour lies under this brilliant critic of a market society. He differed in the definition of liberty from Hume and Smith. For these two, liberty means that a person can do anything, or cannot be forced to do something, so long as he or she does not behave against the public interest. Ferguson thinks this is not enough. As a social animal, a person should behave actively to contribute to the public. Liberty lies in the self-determination to protect oneself by one's own hand. In other words, Ferguson defined modern liberty as participation and autonomy. However, Ferguson is not a Hanna Arendt in the 18th century. As a social scientist, he approved the vitality and industry of vocational life in a modern society. His perspective is therefore much more comprehensive than hers. Recognizing well the importance of private property, free trade and the division of labour in a modern market society whose supremacy to the ancient was evident, Ferguson still remained an acute critic of it from the sociological and political point of view.

Alternative Solutions

If there is reformism, there are revolutionaries, too. Several Scottish thinkers took completely opposing positions against the development of a modern market. Robert Wallace was a minister of the Church of Scotland. He was one of the able opponents of David Hume and famous for his essay on population that was translated into French. Wallace was a student of Edinburgh University in the early 18th century. He was a member of a legendary student club called the Rankenian Club and a friend of prominent figures of the first generation of the Enlightenment, such as Colin MacLaurin, Lord Kames and George Turnbull. He left deistic remarks on religion in these years. After joining the Church hierarchy, he was very active in both church and politics. In later years, he came to sympathize with the radical politics of John Wilkes at the end of the century.

With his mathematical skill elaborated by attending David Gregory's class at Edinburgh University, with his friendship with distinguished scholars and politicians, and with his own convictions, Wallace was an early reformist of the country and in fact he succeeded in establishing the first example of public insurance for widows. His essay on population and the subsequent exchange with David Hume made his name known even to France. The essay was inspired by his critical view against Bernard Mandeville's *The Fable of Bees* and his egalitarian inclinations which preferred social justice and industry to luxury and hierarchy. He was also interested in finding a way to make marriage and agriculture more productive to increase wealth. The former led him to invent the idea that a kind of free and democratic way of marriage would be most productive. For the latter, he concluded that an egalitarian land reform was the most efficient way to bring in wealth.

Wallace's *Prospects* is said to be a source of T. H. Multhus's *An Essay on Population*. But their contexts are very different. Multhus wrote his essay at the end of the century to destroy the radical arguments of William Godwin who published *Political Justice*, a call for a utopian society based upon reason and social justice in the revolutionary period. Wallace's essay has two lines of arguments. The first is the desirability and the reality of a utopian society. The second is, on the contrary, the impractical nature of a utopia. He presented these two inconsistent ideas in the following way: the realization of a utopia is impossible, because it is so perfect and efficient for human happiness and social progress. The success of the advancement of a society is, from Wallace's point of view, evaluated by the rapid growth of population. The growth is very fast in a utopian society and it will soon reach the natural limit, the environment of the earth. Therefore, a utopia will fail not for its internal defects but for its own success. Here we find the surprisingly early cognition of the antagonism between global environment and economic growth.

It is not certain what Wallace really meant to say in this essay. He says at first that a utopia is the perfect system of government that humankind ever imagines. This is the opinion he expressed in an earlier essay on government. He also confirms that there is no obstacle to establishing a utopian regime on this planet given the present nature of the human race. It must work perfectly and successfully. Then he explains why a utopia cannot flourish on the earth. Not the system itself nor the nature of human race, but the present conditions of the planet will threaten the existence of a utopia. If one elaborates his way of reasoning in contemporary contexts, the conclusion will be that not a utopian system, but the liberal global market regime is unrealistic, because it will create, and in fact already has created, environmental disasters in global scale.

It is very likely that Wallace, differing from radical thinkers in the end of the century and socialist writers in the 19th century, literally followed the format of utopian literature. As in the case of Thomas More and Plato in his *Politeia*, a vision of a utopia was not a plan to change an existing government according to it, but a reference point from which a philosopher could see a society critically. In saying that a utopia could not last long on the earth, Wallace denied the reality of it on this planet and affirmed at the same time the theoretical probability of its existence. With his utopian speculation, he succeeded in securing the position to be fundamentally critical against a "commercial society" without being a fanatic dreamer whom he disliked and feared.

Nonetheless, with his imagination and his skill in political arithmetic, Wallace equipped the speculation of an ideal society with more realistic considerations. He was neither a prophet nor a revolutionary. But an idea on utopia endows him with an Archimedes' point to criticize and reverse the existing orders of his society from the outside. His utopian tract was evidence that the Scottish Enlightenment held the context of reformist and revolutionary ideas that were to be expressed later in the writing of William Ogilvie, John Miller and James Mackintosh.

William Ogilvie is lesser known than any other philosophers that appear in this volume. He was a student of Thomas Reid at King's College of Aberdeen and of Adam Smith at Glasgow University. In his political tract published anonymously while he was a professor of King's College, he pushed radical Lockian natural law theory, another source of the radical thinking of Scottish Enlightenment, to an extreme in the following two senses. In the Lockian understanding of property, God allowed people to occupy and utilize land in order to satisfy human needs. Therefore, Ogilvie concludes that every member of a society has a "birth right" to demand a fragment of land on which to live. Not only speculating about the ideal forms of a society, he proceeds to elaborate this basic idea to several concrete policy recommendations, mostly several plans of the redistribution of landed property. He distinguished three kinds of value, or the fertilities of land. Land is fertile because of its nature. Land also has the possibility to become more productive due to improvement in the future. Only productivity already created by investment done by the landowner can be regarded as the owner's "property". The product of the fertilities of other two should belong to public's use. Having so defined the substance of birth right, Ogilvie examines and proposes several policies of practical land reform. Eventually he became a precursor of Lockian radicals in England such as Thomas Spence and Thomas Paine, and of the movements of land reform in the 19th century.

Ogilvie, being an experienced landowner, concluded that the redistribution of land to the poor would not only contribute to the social welfare of citizens, but would also create the necessary condition for stable and favourable economic developments. This argument looks very familiar to North-East Asians today, for the highly praised economic miracles of Japan, South Korea and China were partly based on these kind of agricultural policies, though the reforms were implemented not by democratic governments, but by the American occupation army in Japan, military dictators in South Korea and the communist regime in China. On the contrary, against the apparent seriousness of the intentions of the author, the "birth right" tract of Ogilvie was never actualized in its birth place.

However eccentric it may seem to be, the tract was an attempt to give a solution to the central issue of Scottish social and political thought, especially the issue of how to ease the tension between the market and social cohesion. It gives evidence that radical utopian thinking in Scottish philosophers could be brought to actual political movements. Scottish moral philosophy was not confined to pedagogic practice aimed to raise responsible members of a society. It was the hotbed of reformist ideas, notably seen in the political economy class of Dugald Stewart at the end of the century.

Thomas Reid was recorded in the history of philosophy as the founder of Scottish common sense school and the prominent opponent of David Hume. His fame was, for 21st century readers, unimaginably great by the end of 18th century and the first half of the 19th century. The uniqueness of his socio-political philosophy was hardly recognized until the publication of his manuscripts in the late 1980s, although it must have influenced his students, including Ogilvie and Dugald Stewart. There was a time when Reid was regarded as socially and politically conservative. The recovery of his paper on utopian system has changed our views of

Reid as a social and political philosopher of the Enlightenment forever.

In his utopian tract, Reid pushed the issue of wealth and virtue in the Scottish Enlightenment, the contradictive nature of the market and ethics, to the very extreme. Again in Reid's case, the intention of the author is not self-evident. The paper was only read before his colleagues of Glasgow University at a meeting of the Literary Society of Glasgow and was never published in its complete form. Instead, small extracts of the paper, the introduction and a part of conclusion appeared in a conservative journal with the title, "The Danger of Political Innovation". The asterisks (* page 134, 148) mark the beginning and end of the part originally deleted in the printed edition of the essay. The readers will notice how consciously the editing was done. It is obvious that the publication of the tract was made in order to present Thomas Reid as a conservative who was very afraid of possible political disaster caused by the influence of the French Revolution upon the young people of his country. In fact, Reid was sympathetic to the Revolution. He received a threatening letter because of his appraisal of it and the donation to French parliament. When read in its complete form in this volume, the paper looks to have been written to guide young intellectuals surrounding him to practical reformist policies, warning them that fundamental change in a society can be dangerous without credible evidence and careful experiments. The paper also clearly demonstrates that a utopian system is not unrealistic. Consequently, Reid's position toward the ideal form of a society is very similar to that of Wallace.

When Wallace brought theoretical and practical seriousness to utopian speculation, Reid infused it with the achievements of Scottish Enlightenment, the study of human nature and political economy. He was praised by Dugald Stewart for successfully applying the method of "experimental philosophy" to the study of human nature. He became interested in the issues of political economy when he was in Aberdeen and taught the topic in Glasgow University as the successor of Adam Smith. In his lecture notes, he demonstrates that he had a better understanding of the subject than any other professor of moral philosophy in Scotland except Smith himself.

How desirable and ethically correct the behaviors of the inhabitants of a utopian system may look, the system lacks strong passion to fulfill individuals' desires. It is the main drive of the actors in the market system and the sole propelling force of human behavior that Smith and Stewart presupposed in deducing the functions of the system. Ferguson viewed ambitions as the stimulus to the progress of humanity. With Wallace, Reid at the end of the century thought that something had to replace the self-interest axiom of a market society in a utopian system. He introduced scales of honour and income differentials into the system as an alternative. Then there would be emulation, not competition, among the citizens of a utopia.

For Smith and Reid, the problem of political economy is how to promote the production of national wealth. Wealth is the product of labour and therefore an economic system is the system of the allocation of labour as the main resource of production. For Reid, the question of political economy is to find the most efficient way to allocate labour. His conclusion was that a utopian system was the best system in political economy. His utopia is in fact an ancestor of socialist economy based upon public ownership and central planning. It is a very surprising experience indeed to read such paragraphs written by a Scottish moral philosopher of the 18th century and to find them very similar to the passages from *Das Kapital*.

Perhaps because of being clergy who took the responsibility of managing poor law system, Wallace and Reid shared the same feeling towards the growing gap between the rich and the poor in their society. They used the same expression as found in the English translation of More's *Utopia*, "the beasts of burden", to condemn the rich and demand justice for the poor. In More's original, the phrase appeared in a very impressive passage where the author openly expressed his compassion for the lower ranks of his society forced to live in miserable conditions. Apparently both church men felt the same sentiments in their engagement in the business of social welfare. It is also certain, however, that both welcomed the fruits of the market system. Their philosophical reasoning therefore focused on finding a social and political system to achieve wealth without the present system of inequality and oppression.

Conclusion: Cosmology, Plurality and Locality

So far we have seen 18th century Scottish achievements as having contemporary relevance. Being both for and against a modern market society, 18th century Scottish socio-political thought is very inspiring and has continued to appeal to today's readers. Finally, we will turn our attention to their out-dated and forgotten dimensions.

While Wallace, Ogilvie and Reid were too pessimistic about the self-managing ability of a modern market society, Hume and Smith overlooked the factors that threaten it today. If they could have taken into account the international movement of capital involving the outflow of jobs and the international movement of people themselves, they could have never thought that economic growth and stable social order would have been brought into harmony. It is very natural that Scottish philosophers' scopes were limited by their experience as it was restricted to their century and locality.

There are also paradigmatic limitations that can instantly be noticed in the works of every philosopher in this volume. How broad and universal the perspective of Scottish philosophy of the century was, nobody can deny the fact that it developed within the cultural boundaries of the country and the period. Most of the thinkers were moderate Presbyterians. At most, like Hume and young George Turnbull, they were deists and not atheists. All of them believed in natural theology and the existence of an intelligent Creator of the universe. In other words, their philosophy developed within the framework of the modern European Christian tradition and never stepped out of it.

This limit of scope, apparently narrower than that of the French Enlightenment where outspoken atheists and materialists were actively writing, if seen from a different angle, evidences the uniqueness and contemporary relevance of 18th century thought. As Newtonianism was dominant in the intellectual landscape of the country, every aspect of thinking was connected to the cosmology that had been completely reformed by modern astronomy. This cosmological aspect of 18th century thought is seriously lacking in contemporary political and social thought. Until modern sciences as the cluster of specialized disciplines emerged in the 19th and 20th centuries, the Copernican system could not be separated from "the plurality of the worlds", especially after Galileo found mountains and valleys on the surface of the moon by means of the newly invented telescope. The idea of "the plurality of the worlds" has its origin in the doctrines of ancient Greek philosophers. It was discussed by Christian philosophers in the middle age. In the 18th century the cosmology of modern astronomy made "plurality" mean the existence of other ecosystems on other planets in the universe. Many eminent astronomers believed in the existence of extra-terrestrial intelligent life forms, or at least felt no need to deny the probability of it.[6] Consequently, most Newtonian scientists viewed the idea as an inseparable part of the Newtonian system of the universe. I will quote two long paragraphs from the works of Colin MacLaurin, a natural philosopher, and Adam Ferguson, a moral philosopher, in order to show how different the way of thinking in the Enlightenment was from ours.

The plurality is taken for granted in the famous handbook to Newtonian philosophy written by MacLaurin, the professor of natural philosophy of Edinburgh University. He was a leading Newtonian in Scotland and the greatest British mathematician of the century. In the following quotation, the existence of extra-terrestrial intelligent life forms is not only taken for granted, but also serves to demonstrate the prospects of the future improvement of human intelligence:

> We cannot but take notice of one thing, that appears to have been designed by the author of nature: he has made it impossible for us to have any communication from this earth with the other great bodies of the universe, in our present state; and it is highly probable, that he has likewise cut off all communication betwixt the other planets, and betwixt the different systems. We are able, by telescopes, to discover plains, mountains, precipices, or for cavities in the moon: but who tread those precipices, or for what purposes those great cavities (many of which have a little elevation in the middle) serve, we know not; and at a loss to conceive how this planet, without any atmosphere, vapours, or seas, can serve for like purposes as our earth. We observe sudden and surprising revolutions on the surface of the great planet Jupiter, which would be fatal to the inhabitants of the earth ... It does not appear to be suitable that we should see so far, and have our curiosity so much raised concerning the works of God, only to be disappointed at the end. As man is undoubtedly the chief being upon this globe, and this globe may be no less considerable, in the most valuable respects, than any other in the solar system, and this system, for ought we know, not inferior to any in the universal system so, if we should suppose man to perish, without ever arriving at a more complete knowledge of nature, than the ever arriving at

---

[6]　Frenchman Laplace (1749–1827) wrote in his published in 1796. "Their existence is, at least, extremely probable" (Pierre Simon Laplace, Exposition du système du monde, Paris, 1796).

a more complete knowledge of nature, than the very imperfect one he attains in his present state; by analogy, or parity of reason, we might conclude, that the like desires would be frustrated in the inhabitants of all the other planets and systems; and that the beautiful scheme of nature would never be infolded, but in an exceedingly imperfect manner, to any of them. This, therefore, naturally leads us to consider our present state as only the dawn or beginning of our existence, and as a state of preparation or probation for farther advancement.[7]

The same belief is found in the following excerpt from Adam Ferguson's unpublished papers written in the early 19th century. As the last survivor of the Enlightenment literati, Ferguson constructed his speculations of omnipresent intelligence in the early 19th century on the common cosmological knowledge which MacLaurin displayed. He first asks himself the reason of the existence of vast material universe which modern astronomy has found. Then he calculated the "population" of intelligent beings in the universe from human experience and estimates that it will be two thousand million millions, enough to cover the whole of the universe. He concludes that the populousness of the universe is the basis for human moral advancement, because the idea of the existence and the number of the higher ranks of intelligence encourages people to improve themselves mentally and spiritually by the psychology of emulation:

OF THE COMPARATIVE FORMS OF BEING

The material world being such as we perceive it from afar as well as near indefinitely various and great: What are we to think of the intellectual or world of minds? ...

If thus the scale of estimation be disturbed on earth where the human soul is so perspicuous; no wonder we are ravished with the magnitude and order of a firmament now discovered by the sagacity of men to present many such worlds as we inhabit, while the essence of a superiour form of being for whose use such magnitude of scenery is made has yet, if at all, but faintly or by conjecture dawned upon our sight...

From the magnitude etc. of planets they were guessed to be worlds like this earth, and from their motions this earth was guessed to be a planet like them. Of this there is now no doubt, but when we would go farther and guess they are inhabited, we must admit the probability of great variety as well as analogy in the forms of existence in comparison with that we experience.

---

[7] Colin MacLaurin, *An Account of Sir Isaac Newton's Philosophical Discoveries*, 1748, pp. 390-2.

It is thus that without rejecting the characteristic diversity of forms in nature we apprehend in every planet by which our sun is surrounded a living world analogous to that of which we ourselves make a part on this terrestrial sphere, and in every fixed star a sun like our own environed also with planets revolving in orbits such as we have learned with so much accuracy in all their anomaly vibrations and mutual disturbances. Nor do we sense a limit to this assumption of worlds not to be limited merely by our defect of sight which does not extend beyond a mere corner of universal existence that has no bounds but those of number and space if to such there be any limits.

So great, so numerous are the forms of material existence. To what effect or for what purpose?

This question for ever occurs on our observation of nature, and where it cannot be solved, we are slow of belief in the fact so manifest commonly is the end in all the forms or operations of nature...

Is the universe of body then formed for the sake of mind alone? To us there appears no other end or purpose for which it is made. If so great the corporeal departments of nature, what are we to think of the mental for whose sake those departments are so formed and dispersed throughout the immensity of space? ...

That we may perceive the vanity to number in this instances be it remembered that the human species of any one generation has been reckoned at one thousand millions: if but one hundred generations are supposed to have assed, one hundred thousand millions of souls have already flown from terrestrial source; and if every planet in he solar system has been equally productive, the sum will amount to seven hundred thousand millions; and if every fixed star supposed to be two thousand is but the sign post if a system similar to ours, let imagination try to accompany in thought two thousands millions of millions which figures may in vain be used to express and let the vanquished conception acknowledge that the material world, however great, is still subordinate, and even upon such data as the material world itself can supply must shrink in magnitude as well as in estimation before the world of living and conscious existence whose essence is power and distinction, felicity...

When the aspiring mind recalls the millions of millions and hundred thousands of millions of millions with whom he may now have to contend for distinction, he may possibly shrink in despair. But if he judge aright, the object of a just ambition is not comparative but of an absolute value. That in which the value of existence itself consists is the capacity of happiness, and the happy mind is of the highest value whatever be the number that partakes in the same distinction.

If you perform what in the present moment what you are called upon to do with benignity, diligence and resolution, you are happy.

To this it may be subjoined that the multitude of competitors in the same pursuit will not impede but promote the success.[8]

Astronomy, plurality, political economy and Stoic virtues are consciously mixed together in Ferguson's version of Cicero's "The dream of Scipio", so that it illustrates the prospect of human moral progress within the framework of early modern science's cosmology. The way Enlightenment thinkers looked at humanity is not the same as ours. Based upon the Semitic religious tradition of an omnipotent God, they were able to put together the image of an infinite universe and the superiority of the mind above the material world. Thomas Reid taught in his lectures on moral philosophy at Glasgow University that human nature is only one empirical subject available to us from which we understood how mind works. In this context, the mind means universal intelligence, whose owners include God, angels and the probable inhabitants of other planets and other solar systems. These Semitic-Christian ideas and cosmological imaginations, as a way of thinking, enabled Enlightenment philosophers to grasp humanity in universal perspective.

It is easy to laugh at these speculations as the absurd products of pseudo-science in the early modern period. But this embeddedness of socio-political thought into cosmology could inspire our rethinking of humanity in the 21st century, when the unprecedented advancement of science and technology, together with the increasing conflicts between cultures and civilizations, endangers humanity's traditional ideals. We are living in an age when the view of the universe is dramatically changing beyond the imagination of both ancient and modern philosophers. Genetic research has demonstrated that humans share many genes with an octopus, a cockroach and a paramecium, not to mention that a chimpanzee is genetically almost a human being. Scientists are not sure whether the future development of artificial intelligence can create a machine that thinks and feels like a human or not. We also do not know where genetic technology will lead us. But it is certain that the concept of intelligence and "humanity" must be broadened, transcending the narrow defini-

---

[8] *From The Papers of Adam Ferguson*, owned by Edinburgh University Library, first published in Yasuo Amoh (ed.), Adam Ferguson, *Collection of Essays*, Rinsen Book Co., Kyoto, 1996, pp. 92-5.

tion of humanity in the 19th and 20th centuries, which is the creation of cultural and historical localities of modern Europe.

Ferguson's speculation is a typical response of a moral philosopher to the changing view of nature and humanity in the 18th century within the given settings of West European cultural values. His idea of mind and intelligence was at least not confined to the geographical localities of the human race in the universe.[9] Our task is how to proceed beyond out-dated ideas like liberalism and socialism upon different values and ethics and to find new syntheses of our belief system and science. The achievements and limitations of 18th century Scottish socio-political thoughts could become, not an answer, but a catalyst to this endeavour.

*

Acknowledgement

I would like to thank here to my friends and students at Nagoya University, Dr. Natsuko Fukuda, Ms. Nozomi Takemae and Ms. Yuka Sogawa for scanning, typing and correcting the texts in this volume.

---

[9] This modernized concept of "universal intelligence" of the Enlightenment was able to transcend their cultural boundaries. The astronomical work of John Keil, a Scottish Newtonian at Oxford, played the crucial role in introducing Copernican theory to pre-modern Japan. The 18th century Japanese translation of his book on Newtonian astronomy says: "The space is so vast and boundless. There is no reason that only our sun has planets round itself. Other stars must have other planets as our five ones. Why is our earth the only place of the inhabitance of people and things, among all these innumerable planets? In other worlds of our planets, and in other worlds of the planets of other suns, there is no reason that no inhabitants live, even if their shapes and figures are different from us." (Shizuki Tadao (1760–1806), *A New Book of Astronomy* (Rekishou Sinsho), 1798–1802, p. 129, 1969 edition.)

An introduction to Newtonian astronomy in the early 19th century says: "The earth is one of the planets in the heaven. Be aware that all the planets and the moons are immense inhabited worlds. This is the point why western philosophers teach Copernican system" (Yoshio Josan, *An Illustrated Introduction to Far-Western Astronomy with a view to Physics* (Rigaku Nyushiki Ensei Kanshou Zusetsu), 1828). These Japanese Newtonians confidently maintained their Confucius philosophy and both concluded that Eastern philosophy is superior to Western philosophy and religion. But they had no difficulty in accepting the view of the vast universe full of intelligent life forms.

I. The Discovery of Modern Market Society

One

David Hume
(1711–1776)

OF THE ORIGINAL CONTRACT (1748)

As no party, in the present age, can well support itself without a philosophical or speculative system of principles annexed to its political or practical one, we accordingly find, that each of the factions into which this nation is divided has reared up a fabric of the former kind, in order to protect and cover that scheme of actions which it pursues. The people being commonly very rude builders, especially in this speculative way, and more especially still when actuated by party zeal, it is natural to imagine that their workmanship must be a little unshapely, and discover evident marks of that violence and hurry in which it was raised. The one party, by tracing up government to the Deity, endeavours to render it so sacred and inviolate, that it must be little less than sacrilege, however tyrannical it may become, to touch or invade it in the smallest article. The other party, by founding government altogether on the consent of the people, suppose that there is a kind of original contract, by which the subjects have tacitly reserved the power of resisting their sovereign, whenever they find themselves aggrieved by that authority with which they have, for certain purposes, voluntarily intrusted him. These are the speculative principles of the two parties, and these, too, are the practical consequences deduced from them.

I shall venture to affirm, *that both these systems of speculative principles are just, though not in the sense intended by the parties: and, That both the schemes of practical consequences are prudent, though not in the extremes to which each party, in opposition to the other, has commonly endeavoured to carry them.*

That the Deity is the ultimate author of all government, will never be denied by any, who admit a general providence, and allow, that all events in the universe are conducted by an uniform plan, and directed to wise purposes. As it is impossible for the human race to subsist, at least in any comfortable or secure state, without the protection of government, this institution must certainly have been intended by that beneficent Being, who means the good of all his creatures: and as it has universally, in fact, taken place in all countries, and all ages, we may conclude, with still greater certainty, that it was intended by that omniscient Being, who can never be deceived by any event or operation. But since he gave rise to it, not by any particular or miraculous interposition, but by his concealed and universal efficacy, a sovereign cannot, properly speaking, be called his vicegerent in any other sense than every power or force, being derived from him, may be said to act by his commission. Whatever actually happens is comprehended in the general plan or intention of Providence; nor has the greatest and most lawful prince any more reason, upon that account, to plead a peculiar sacredness or inviolable authority, than an inferior magistrate, or even an usurper, or even a robber and a pirate. The same Divine Superintendent, who, for wise purposes, invested a Titus or a Trajan with authority, did also, for purposes no doubt equally wise, though unknown, bestow power on a Borgia or an Angria. The same causes, which gave rise to the sovereign power in every state, established likewise every petty jurisdiction in it, and every limited authority. A constable, therefore, no less than a king, acts by a divine commission, and possesses an indefeasible right.

When we consider how nearly equal all men are in their bodily force, and even in their mental powers and faculties, till cultivated by education, we must necessarily allow, that nothing but their own consent could at first associate them together and subject them to any authority. The people, if we trace government to its first origin in the woods and deserts, are the source of all power and jurisdiction, and voluntarily, for the sake of peace and order, abandoned their native liberty, and received laws from their equal and companion. The conditions upon which they were willing to submit, were either expressed, or were so clear and obvious that it might well be esteemed superfluous to express them. If this, then, be meant by the original contract, it cannot be denied, that all government is, at first, founded on a contract, and that the most ancient rude combinations of mankind were formed chiefly by that principle. In vain are we asked in what records this charter of our liberties is registered. It was not written on parchment, nor yet on leaves or barks of trees. It preceded the use of writing, and all the other civilized arts of life. But we trace it plainly in the nature of man and in the equality, or something approaching equality, which we find in all the individuals of that species. The force, which now prevails, and which is founded on fleets and armies, is plainly political, and derived from authority, the effect of established government. A man's natural force consists only in the vigour of his limbs, and the firmness of his courage; which could never subject multitudes to the command of one. Nothing but their own consent, and their sense of the advantages resulting from peace and order, could have had that influence.

Yet even this consent was long very imperfect, and could not be the basis of a regular administration. The chieftain, who had probably acquired his influence during the continuance of war, ruled more by persuasion than command; and till he could employ force to reduce the refractory and disobedient, the society could scarcely be said to have attained a state of civil government. No compact or agreement, it is evident, was expressly formed for general submission; an idea far beyond the comprehension of savages: each exertion of authority in the chieftain must have been particular, and called forth by the present exigencies of the case: the sensible utility, resulting from his interposition, made these exertions become daily more frequent; and their frequency gradually produced an habitual, and, if you please to call it so, a voluntary, and therefore precarious, acquiescence in the people.

But philosophers who have embraced a party (if that be not a contradiction in terms), are not contended with these concessions. They assert, not only that government in its earliest infancy arose from consent, or rather the voluntary acquiescence of the people; but also that, even at present, when it has attained its full maturity, it rests on no other foundation. They affirm, that all men are still born equal, and owe allegiance to no prince or government, unless bound by the obligation and sanction of a *promise*. And as no man, without some equivalent, would forego the advantages of his native liberty, and subject himself to the will of another, this promise is always understood to be conditional, and imposes on him no obligation, unless he meet with justice and protection from his sovereign. These advantages the sovereign promises him in return; and if he fail in the execution, he has broken, on his part, the articles of engagement, and has thereby freed his subject from all obligations to allegiance. Such, according to these philosophers, is the foundation of authority in every government, and such the right of resistance possessed by every subject.

But would these reasoners look abroad into the world, they would meet with nothing that, in the least, corresponds to their ideas, or can warrant so refined and philosophical a system. On the contrary, we find everywhere princes who claim their subjects as their property, and assert their independent right of sovereignty, from conquest or succession. We find also everywhere subjects who acknowledge this right in their prince, and suppose themselves born under obligations of obedience to a certain sovereign, as much as under the ties of reverence and duty to certain parents. These connections are always conceived to be equally independent of our consent, in Persia and China, in France and Spain, and even in Holland and England, wherever the doctrines above mentioned have not been carefully inculcated. Obedience or subjection becomes so familiar, that most men never make any inquiry about its origin or cause, more than about the principle of gravity, resistance, or the most universal laws of nature. Or if curiosity ever move them, as soon as they learn that they themselves and their ancestors have, for several ages, or from time immemorial, been subject to such a form of government or such a family, they immediately acquiesce, and acknowledge their obligation to allegiance. Were you to preach, in most parts of the world, that political connections are founded altogether on voluntary consent or a mutual promise, the magistrate would soon imprison you as seditious for loosening the ties of obedience; if your friends did not before shut you up as delirious, for advancing such absurdities. It is strange that an act of the mind, which every individual is supposed to have formed, and after he came to the use of reason too, otherwise it could have no authority; that this act, I say, should be so much unknown to all of them, that over the face of the whole earth, there scarcely remain any traces or memory of it.

But the contract, on which government is founded, is said to be the *original contract*; and consequently may be supposed too old to fall under the knowledge of the present generation. If the agreement, by which savage men first associated and conjoined their force, be here meant, this is acknowledged to be real; but being so ancient, and being obliterated by a thousand changes of government and princes, it cannot now be supposed to retain any authority. If we would say any thing to the purpose, we must assert, that every particular government which is lawful, and which imposes any duty of allegiance on the subject, was, at first, founded on consent and a voluntary compact. But, besides that this supposes the consent of the fathers to bind the children, even to the most remote generations (which republican writers will never allow), besides this, I say, it is not justified by history or experience in any age or country of the world.

Almost all the governments which exist at present, or of which there remains any record in story, have been founded originally, either on usurpation or conquest, or both, without any pretence of a fair consent or voluntary subjection of the people. When an artful and bold man is placed at the head of an army or faction, it is often easy for him, by employing, sometimes violence, sometimes false pretences, to establish his dominion over a people a hundred times more numerous than his partisans. He allows no such open communication, that his enemies can know, with certainty, their number or force. He gives them no leisure to assemble together in a body to oppose him. Even all those who are the instruments of his usurpation may wish his fall; but their ignorance of each other's intention keeps them in awe, and is the sole cause of his security. By such arts as these many governments have been established; and this is all the *original contract* which they have to boast of.

The face of the earth is continually changing, by the increase of small kingdoms into great empires, by the dissolution of great empires into smaller kingdoms, by the planting of colonies, by the migration of tribes. Is there any thing discoverable in all these events but force and violence? Where is the mutual agreement or voluntary association so much talked of?

Even the smoothest way by which a nation may receive a foreign master, by marriage or a will, is not extremely honourable for the people; but supposes them to be disposed of like a dowry or a legacy, according to the pleasure or interest of their rulers.

But where no force interposes, and election takes place, what is this election so highly vaunted? It is either the combination of a few great men, who decide for the whole, and will allow of no opposition; or it is the fury of a multitude, that follow a seditious ringleader, who is not known, perhaps, to a dozen among them, and who owes his advancement merely to his own impudence, or to the momentary caprice of his fellows.

Are these disorderly elections, which are rare too, of such mighty authority as to be the only lawful foundation of all government and allegiance?

In reality there is not a more terrible event than a total dissolution of government, which gives liberty to the multitude, and makes the determination or choice of a new establishment depend upon a number, which nearly approaches to that of the body of the people: for it never comes entirely to the whole body of them. Every wise man then wishes to see, at the head of a powerful and obedient army, a general who may speedily seize the prize, and give to the people a master which they are so unfit to choose for themselves; so little correspondent is fact and reality to those philosophical notions.

Let not the establishment at the *Revolution* deceive us, or make us so much in love with a philosophical origin to government, as to imagine all others monstrous and irregular. Even that event was far from corresponding to these refined ideas. It was only the succession, and that only in the regal part of the government, which was then changed: and it was only the majority of seven hundred, who determined that change for near ten millions. I doubt not, indeed, but the bulk of those ten millions acquiesced willingly in the determination: but was the matter left, in the least, to their choice? Was it not justly supposed to be, from that moment, decided, and every man punished, who refused to submit to the new sovereign? How otherwise could the matter have ever been brought to any issue or conclusion?

The republic of Athens was, I believe, the most extensive democracy that we read of in history: yet if we make the requisite allowances for the women, the slaves, and the strangers, we shall find, that that establishment was not at first made, nor any law ever voted, by a tenth part of those who were bound to pay obedience to it; not to mention the islands and foreign dominions, which the Athenians claimed as theirs by right of conquest. And as it is well known that popular assemblies in that city were always full of license and disorder, notwithstanding the institutions and laws by which they were checked; how much more disorderly must they prove, where they form not the established constitution, but meet tumultuously on the dissolution of the ancient government, in order to give rise to a new one? How chimerical must it be to talk of a choice in such circumstances?

The Achaeans enjoyed the freest and most perfect democracy of all antiquity; yet they employed force to oblige some cities to enter into their league, as we learn from Polybius.

Harry IV and Harry VII of England, had really no title to the throne but a parliamentary election; yet they never would acknowledge it, lest they should thereby weaken their authority. Strange, if the only real foundation of all authority be consent and promise?

It is in vain to say that all governments are, or should be, at first founded on popular consent, as much as the necessity of human affairs will admit. This favours entirely my pretension. I maintain, that human affairs will never admit of this consent, seldom of the appearance of it; but that conquest or usurpation, that is, in plain terms, force, by dissolving the ancient governments, is the origin of almost all the new ones which were ever established in the world. And that in the few cases where consent may seem to have taken place, it was commonly so irregular, so confined, or so much intermixed either with fraud or violence, that it cannot have any great authority.

My intention here is not to exclude the consent of the people from being one just foundation of government. Where it has place, it is surely the best and most sacred of any. I only contend, that it has very seldom had place in any degree, and never almost in its full extent; and that, therefore, some other foundation of government must also be admitted.

Were all men possessed of so inflexible a regard to justice, that of themselves they would totally abstain from the properties of others; they had for ever remained in a state of absolute liberty, without subjection to any magistrate or political society: but this is a state of perfection of which human nature is justly deemed incapable. Again, were all men possessed of so perfect an understanding as always to know their own interests, no form of government had ever been submitted to but what was established on consent, and was fully canvassed by every member of the society: but this state of perfection is likewise much superior to human nature. Reason, history, and experience show us, that all political societies have had an origin much less accurate and regular; and were one to choose a period of time when the people's consent was the least regarded in public transactions, it would be precisely on the establishment of a new government. In a settled constitution, their inclinations are often consulted; but during the fury of revolutions, conquests, and public convulsions, military force or political craft usually decides the controversy.

When a new government is established, by whatever means, the people are commonly dissatisfied with it, and pay obedience more from fear and necessity, than from any idea of allegiance or of moral obligation. The prince is watchful and jealous, and must carefully guard against every beginning or appearance of insurrection. Time, by degrees, removes all these difficulties, and accustoms the nation to regard, as their lawful or native princes, that family which at first they considered as usurpers or foreign conquerors. In order to found this opinion, they have no recourse to any notion of voluntary consent or promise, which, they know, never was, in this case, either expected or demanded. The original establishment was formed by violence, and submitted to from necessity. The subsequent administration is also supported by power, and acquiesced in by the people, not as a matter of choice, but of obligation. They imagine not that their consent gives their prince a title: but they willingly consent, because they think, that, from long possession, he has acquired a title, independent of their choice or inclination.

Should it be said, that, by living under the dominion of a prince which one might leave, every individual has given a *tacit* consent to his authority, and promised him obedience; it may be answered, that such an implied consent can only have place where a man imagines that the matter depends on his choice. But where he thinks (as all mankind do who are born under established governments) that, by his birth, he owes allegiance to a certain prince or certain form of government; it would be absurd to infer a consent or choice, which he expressly, in this case, renounces and disclaims.

Can we seriously say, that a poor peasant or artisan has a free choice to leave his country, when he knows no foreign language or manners, and lives, from day to day, by the small wages which he acquires? We may as well assert that a man, by remaining in a vessel, freely consents to the dominion of the master; though he was carried on board while asleep, and must leap into the ocean and perish, the moment he leaves her.

What if the prince forbid his subjects to quit his dominions; as in Tiberius's time, it was regarded as a crime in a Roman knight that he had attempted to fly to the Parthians, in order to escape the tyranny of that emperor? Or as the ancient Muscovites prohibited all traveling under pain of death? And did a prince observe, that many of his subjects were seized with the frenzy of migrating to foreign countries, he would, doubtless, with great reason and justice, restrain them, in order to prevent the depopulation of his own kingdom. Would he forfeit the allegiance of all his subjects by so wise and reasonable a law? Yet the freedom of their choice is surely, in that case, ravished from them.

A company of men, who should leave their native country, in order to people some uninhabited region, might dream of recovering their native freedom, but they would soon find, that their prince still laid claim to them, and called them his subjects, even in their new settlement. And in this he would but act conformably to the common ideas of mankind.

The truest *tacit* consent of this kind that is ever observed, is when a foreigner settles in any country, and is beforehand acquainted with the prince, and government, and laws, to which he must submit: yet is his allegiance, though more voluntary, much less expected or depended on, than that of a natural born subject. On the contrary, his native prince still asserts a claim to him. And if he punish not the renegade, when he seizes him in war with his new prince's commission; this clemency is not founded on the municipal law, which in all countries condemns the prisoner; but on the consent of princes, who have agreed to this indulgence, in order to prevent reprisals.

Did one generation of men go off the stage at once, and another succeed, as is the case with silkworms and butterflies, the new race, if they had sense enough to choose their government, which surely is never the case with men, might voluntarily, and by general consent, establish their own form of civil polity, without any regard to the laws or precedents which prevailed among their ancestors. But as human society is in perpetual flux, one man every hour going out of the world, another coming into it, it is necessary, in order to preserve stability in government, that the new brood should conform themselves to the established constitution, and nearly follow the path which their fathers, treading in the footsteps of theirs, had marked out to them. Some innovations must necessarily have place in every human institution; and it is happy where the enlightened genius of the age give these a direction to the side of reason, liberty, and justice: but violent innovations no individual is entitled to make: they are even dangerous to be attempted by the legislature: more ill than good is ever to be expected from them: and if history affords examples to the contrary, they are not to be drawn into precedent, and are only to be regarded as proofs, that the science of politics affords few rules, which will not admit of some exception, and which may not sometimes be controlled by fortune and accident. The violent innovations in the reign of Henry VIII proceeded from an imperious monarch, seconded by the appearance of legislative authority: those in the reign of Charles I were derived from faction and fanaticism; and both of them have proved happy in the issue. But even the former were long the source of many disorders, and still more dangers; and if the measures of allegiance were to be taken from the latter, a total anarchy must have place in human society, and a final period at once be put to every government.

Suppose that an usurper, after having banished his lawful prince and royal family, should establish his dominion for ten or a dozen years in any country, and should preserve so exact a discipline in his troops, and so regular a disposition in his garrisons that no insurrection had ever been raised, or even murmur heard against his administration: can it be asserted that the people, who in their hearts abhor his treason, have tacitly consented to his authority, and promised him allegiance, merely because, from necessity, they live under his dominion? Suppose again their native prince restored, by means of an army, which he levies in foreign countries: they receive him with joy and exultation, and show plainly with what reluctance they had submitted to any other yoke. I may now ask, upon what foundation the prince's title stands? Not on popular consent surely: for though the people willingly acquiesce in his authority, they never imagine that their consent made him sovereign. They consent, because they apprehend him to be already by birth, their lawful sovereign. And as to tacit consent, which may now be inferred from their living under his dominion, this is no more than what they formerly gave to the tyrant and usurper.

When we assert that all lawful government arises from the consent of the people, we certainly do them a great deal more honour than they deserve, or even expect and desire from us. After the Roman dominions became too unwieldy for the republic to govern them, the people over the whole world were extremely grateful to Augustus for that authority which by violence, he had established over them; and they showed an equal disposition to submit to the successor whom he left them by his last will and testament. It was afterwards their misfortune that there never was, in one family, any long regular succession; but that their line of princes was continually broken, either by private assassinations or public rebellions. The *praetorian* bands, on the failure of every family, set up one emperor; the legions in the East a second; those in Germany, perhaps, a third; and, the sword alone could decide the controversy. The condition of the people in that mighty monarchy was to be lamented not because the choice of the emperor was never left to them, for that was impracticable, but because they never fell under any succession of masters who might regularly follow each other. As to the violence, and wars, and, bloodshed, occasioned by every new settlement, these were not blamable, because they were inevitable.

The house of Lancaster ruled in this island about sixty years; yet the partisans of the white rose seemed daily to multiply in England. The present establishment has taken place during a still longer period. Have all views of right in another family been utterly extinguished, even though scarce any man now alive had arrived at the years of discretion when it was expelled, or could have consented to its dominion, or have promised its allegiance? — a sufficient indication, surely, of the general sentiment of mankind on this head. For we blame not the partisans of the abdicated family merely on account of the long time during which they have preserved their imaginary loyalty. We blame them for adhering to a family which we affirm has been justly expelled, and which, from the moment the new settlement took place, had forfeited all title to authority.

But would we have a more regular, at least a more philosophical refutation of this principle of an original contract, or popular consent, perhaps the following observations may suffice.

All *moral* duties may be divided into two kinds. The *first* are those to which men are impelled by a natural instinct or immediate propensity which operates on them, independent of all ideas of obligation, and of all views either to public or private utility. Of this nature are love of children, gratitude to benefactors, pity to the unfortunate. When we reflect on the advantage which results to society from such humane instincts, we pay them the just tribute of moral approbation and esteem: but the person actuated by them feels their power and influence antecedent to any such reflection.

The *second* kind of moral duties are such as are not supported by any original instinct of nature, but are performed entirely from a sense of obligation, when we consider the necessities of human society, and the impossibility of supporting it, if these duties were neglected. It is thus *justice*, or a regard to the property of others, *fidelity*, or the observance of promises, become obligatory, and acquire an authority over mankind. For as it is evident that every man loves himself better than any other person, he is naturally impelled to extend his acquisitions as much as possible; and nothing can restrain him in this propensity but reflection and experience, by which he learns the pernicious effects of that license, and the total dissolution of society which must ensue from it. His original inclination, therefore, or instinct, is here checked and restrained by a subsequent judgment or observation.

The case is precisely the same with the political or civil duty of *allegiance* as with the natural duties of justice and fidelity. Our primary instincts lead us either to indulge ourselves in unlimited freedom, or to seek dominion over others; and it is reflection only which engages us to sacrifice such strong passions to the interests of peace and public order. A small degree of experience and observation suffices to teach us, that society cannot possibly be maintained without the authority of magistrates, and that this authority must soon fall into contempt where exact obedience is not paid to it. The observation of these general and obvious interests is the source of all allegiance, and of that moral obligation which we attribute to it.

What necessity, therefore, is there to found the duty of *allegiance*, or obedience to magistrates, on that of *fidelity*, or a regard to promises, and to suppose that it is the consent of each individual which subjects him to government, when it appears that both allegiance and fidelity stand precisely on the same foundation, and are both submitted to by mankind, on account of the apparent interests and necessities of human society? We are bound to obey our sovereign, it is said, because we have given a tacit promise to that purpose. But why are we bound to observe our promise? It must here be asserted, that the commerce and intercourse of mankind, which are of such mighty advantage, can have no security where men pay no regard to their engagements. In like manner may it be said that men could not live at all in society, at least in a civilized society, without laws, and magistrates, and judges, to prevent the encroachments of the strong upon the weak, of the violent upon the just and equitable. The obligation to allegiance being of like force and authority with the obligation to fidelity, we gain nothing by resolving the one into the other. The general interests or necessities of society are sufficient to establish both.

If the reason be asked of that obedience which we are bound to pay to government, I readily answer, *because society could not otherwise subsist*; and this answer is clear and intelligible to all mankind. Your answer is, *because we should keep our word*. But besides that nobody, till trained in a philosophical system, can either comprehend or relish this answer; besides this, I say, you find yourself embarrassed when it is asked, *Why we are bound to keep our word?* Nor can you give any answer but what would immediately, without any circuit, have accounted for our obligation to allegiance.

But *to whom is allegiance due, and who is our lawful sovereign?* This question is often the most difficult of any, and liable to infinite discussions. When people are so happy that they can answer, *Our present sovereign, who inherits, in a direct line, from ancestors that have governed us for many ages,* this answer admits of no reply, even though historians, in tracing up to the remotest antiquity the origin of that royal family, may find, as commonly happens, that its first authority was derived from usurpation and violence. It is confessed that private justice, or the abstinence from the properties of others, is a most cardinal virtue. Yet reason tells us that there is no property in durable objects, such as land or houses, when carefully examined in passing from hand to hand, but must, in some period, have been founded on fraud and injustice. The necessities of human society, neither in private nor public life, will allow of such an accurate inquiry; and there is no virtue or moral duty but what may, with facility, be refined away, if we indulge a false philosophy in sifting and scrutinizing it, by every captious rule of logic, in every light or position in which it may be placed.

The questions with regard to private property have filled infinite volumes of law and philosophy, if in both we add the commentators to the original text; and in the end we may safely pronounce, that many of the rules there established are uncertain, ambiguous, and arbitrary. The like opinion may be formed with regard to the succession and rights of princes, and forms of government. Several cases no doubt occur, especially in the infancy of any constitution, which admit of no determination from the laws of justice and equity; and our historian, Rapin pretends, that the controversy between Edward the Third and Philip de Valois was of this nature, and could be decided only by an appeal to heaven, that is, by war and violence...

In an absolute government, when there is no legal prince who has a title to the throne, it may safely be determined to belong to the first occupant. Instances of this kind are but too frequent, especially in the eastern monarchies. When any race of princes expires, the will or destination of the last sovereign will be regarded as a title. Thus the edict of Louis XIV, who called the bastard princes to the succession in case of the failure of all the legitimate princes, would, in such an event, have some authority. Thus the will of Charles the Second disposed of the whole Spanish monarchy. The cession of the ancient proprietor, especially when joined to conquest, is likewise deemed a good title. The general obligation, which binds us to government, is the interest and necessities of society; and this obligation is very strong. The determination of it to this or that particular prince, or form of government, is frequently more uncertain and dubious. Present possession has considerable authority in these cases, and greater than in private property; because of the disorders which attend all revolutions and changes of government.

We shall only observe, before we conclude, that though an appeal to general opinion may justly, in the speculative sciences of metaphysics, natural philosophy, or astronomy, be deemed unfair and inconclusive, yet in all questions with regard to morals, as well as criticism, there is really no other standard by which any controversy can ever be decided. And nothing is a clearer proof, that a theory of this kind is erroneous, than to find that it leads to paradoxes repugnant to the common sentiments of mankind, and to the practice and opinion of all nations and all ages. The doctrine which founds all lawful government on an *original contract* or consent of the people, is plainly of this kind; nor has the most noted of its partisans, in prosecution of it, scrupled to affirm, *that absolute monarchy is inconsistent with civil society, and so can be no form of civil government at all; and that the supreme power in a state cannot take from any man, by taxes and impositions, any part of his property, without his own consent or that of his representatives.* What authority any moral reasoning can have, which leads into opinions so wide of the general practice of mankind, in every place but this single kingdom, it is easy to determine.

The only passage I meet with in antiquity, where the obligation of obedience to government is ascribed to a promise, is in Plato's Crito; where Socrates refuses to escape from prison, because he had tacitly promised to obey the laws. Thus he builds a Tory consequence of passive obedience on a Whig foundation of the original contract.

New discoveries are not to be expected in these matters. If scarce any man, till very lately, ever imagined that government was founded on compact, it is certain that it cannot, in general, have any such foundation.

The crime of rebellion among the ancients was commonly expressed by the terms *neoterizein, novas res moliri*.

OF REFINEMENT IN THE ARTS (1752)

Luxury is a word of an uncertain signification, and may be taken in a good as well as in a bad sense. In general it means great refinement in the gratification of the senses; and any degree of it may be innocent or blamable, according to the age, or country or condition of the person. The bounds between the virtue and the vice cannot here be exactly fixed more than in other moral subjects. To imagine, that the gratifying of any sense, or the indulging of any delicacy in meat, drink, or apparel, is of itself a vice can never enter into a head, that is not disordered by the frenzies of enthusiasm. I have indeed heard of a monk abroad, who, because the windows of his cell opened upon a noble prospect, made *a covenant with his eyes* never to turn that way, or receive so sensuous a gratification. And such is the crime of drinking Champagne or Burgundy, preferably to small beer or porter. These indulgences are only vices, when they are pursued at the expense of some virtue, as liberality or charity; in like manner as they are follies, when for them a man ruins his fortune, and reduces himself to want and beggary. Where they entrench upon no virtue, but leave ample subject whence to provide for friends, family, and every proper object of generosity or compassion, they are entirely innocent, and have in every age been acknowledged such by almost all moralists. To be entirely occupied with the luxury of the table, for instance, without any relish for the pleasures of ambition, study, or conversation, is a mark of stupidity, and is incompatible with any vigour of temper or genius. To confine one's expense entirely to such a gratification, without regard to friends or family, is an indication of a heart destitute of humanity or benevolence. But if a man reserve time sufficient for all laudable pursuits, and money sufficient for all generous purposes, he is free from every shadow of blame or reproach.

Since luxury may be considered either as innocent or blamable, one may be surprised at those preposterous opinions which have been entertained concerning it; while men of libertine principles bestow praises even on vicious luxury, and represent it as highly advantageous to society; and, on the other hand, men of severe morals blame even the most innocent luxury, and represent it as the source of all the corruptions, disorders, and factions incident to civil government. We shall here endeavour to correct both these extremes, by proving, *first*, that the ages of refinement are both the happiest and most virtuous; *secondly*, that wherever luxury ceases to be innocent, it also ceases to be beneficial; and when carried a degree too far is a quality pernicious, though perhaps not the most pernicious, to political society.

To prove the first point, we need but consider the effects of refinement both on *private* and on *public* life. Human happiness, according to the most received notions, seems to consist in three ingredients: action, pleasure, and indolence: and though these ingredients ought to be mixed in different proportions, according to the particular disposition of the person; yet no one ingredient can be entirely wanting, without destroying, in some measure, the *relish* of the whole composition. Indolence or repose, indeed, seems not of itself to contribute much to our enjoyment; but, like sheep, is requisite as an indulgence, to the weakness of human nature, which cannot support an uninterrupted course of business or pleasure. That quick march of the spirits, which takes a man from himself, and chiefly gives satisfaction, does in the end exhaust the mind, and requires some intervals of repose, which, though agreeable for a moment, yet, if prolonged, beget a languor and lethargy, that destroy all enjoyment. Education, custom, and example, have a mighty influence in turning the mind to any of these pursuits; and it must be owned that, where they promote a relish for action and pleasure, they are so favourable to human happiness. In times when industry and the arts flourish, men are kept in perpetual occupation, and enjoy, as their reward, the occupation itself, as well as those pleasures which are the fruit of their labour. The mind acquires new vigour; enlarges its powers and faculties; and, by an assiduity in honest industry, both satisfies its natural appetites, and prevents the growth of unnatural ones, which commonly spring up, when nourished by ease and idleness. Banish those arts from society, you deprive men both of action and of pleasure; and, leaving nothing but indolence in their place, you even destroy the relish of indolence, which never is agreeable, but when it succeeds to labour, and recruits the spirits, exhausted by too much application and fatigue.

Another advantage of industry and of refinements in the mechanical arts is that they commonly produce some refinements in the liberal; nor can one be carried to perfection, without being accompanied, in some degree, with the other. The same age which produces great philosophers and politicians, renowned generals and poets, usually abounds with skilful weavers, and ship-carpenters. We cannot reasonably expect that a piece of woolen cloth will be wrought to perfection in a nation which is ignorant of astronomy, or where ethics are neglected. The spirit of the age affects all the arts, and the minds of men being once roused from their lethargy, and put into a fermentation, turn themselves on all sides, and carry improvements into every art and science. Profound ignorance is totally banished, and men enjoy the privilege of rational creatures, to think as well as to act, to cultivate the pleasures of the mind as well as those of the body.

The more these refined arts advance, the more sociable men become: nor is it possible, that, when enriched with science, and possessed of a fund of conversation, they should be contented to remain in solitude, or live with their fellow-citizens in that distant manner, which is peculiar to ignorant and barbarous nations. They flock into cities; love to receive and communicate knowledge; to show their wit or their breeding; their taste in conversation or living, in clothes or furniture. Curiosity allures the wise; vanity the foolish; and pleasure both. Particular clubs and societies are everywhere formed: both sexes meet in an easy and sociable manner; and the tempers of men, as well as their behaviour, refine apace. So that, beside the improvements which they receive from knowledge and the liberal arts, it is impossible but they must feel an increase of humanity, from the very habit of conversing together, and contributing to each other's pleasure and entertainment. Thus *industry, knowledge,* and *humanity*, are linked together, by an indissoluble chain, and are found, from experience as well as reason, to be peculiar to the more polished, and, what are commonly denominated, the more luxurious ages.

Nor are these advantages attended with disadvantages that bear any proportion to them. The more men refine upon pleasure, the less will they indulge in excesses of any kind; because nothing is more destructive to true pleasure than such excesses. One may safely affirm, that the Tartars are oftener guilty of beastly gluttony, when they feast on their dead horses, than European courtiers with all their refinement of cookery. And if libertine love or even infidelity to the marriage bed be more frequent in polite ages, when it is often regarded only as a piece of gallantry; drunkenness on the other hand, is much less common; a vice more odious, and more pernicious, both to mind and body...

But industry, knowledge, and humanity, are not advantageous in private life alone; they diffuse their beneficial influence on the *public,* and render the government as great and flourishing as they make individuals happy and prosperous. The increase and consumption of all the commodities, which serve to the ornament and pleasure of life, are advantages to society; because, at the same time that they multiply those innocent gratifications to individuals they are a kind of storehouse of labour, which, in the exigencies of state, may be turned to the public service. In a nation where there is no demand for such superfluities, men sink into indolence, lose all enjoyment of life and are useless to the public, which cannot maintain or support its fleets and armies from the industry of such slothful members.

The bounds of all the European kingdoms are, at present, nearly the same they were two hundred years ago. But what a difference is there in the power and grandeur of those kingdoms? Which can be ascribed to nothing but the increase of art and industry. When Charles VIII of France invaded Italy, he carried with him about 20,000 men; yet this armament so exhausted the nation, as we learn from Guicciardin, that for some years it was not able to make so great an effort. The late king of France, in time of war, kept in pay above 400,000 men; though from Mazarine's death to his own he was engaged in a course of wars that lasted nearly thirty years.

This industry is much promoted by the knowledge inseparable from ages of art and refinement; as, on the other hand, this knowledge enables the public to make the best advantage of the industry of its subjects. Laws, order, police, discipline; these can never be carried to any degree of perfection, before human reason has refined itself by exercise, and by an application to the more vulgar arts, at least of commerce and manufacture. Can we expect that a government will be well modeled by a people, who know not how to make a spinning wheel, or to employ a loom to advantage? Not to mention that all ignorant ages are infected with superstition, which throws the government off its bias, and disturbs men in the pursuit of their interest and happiness. Knowledge in the arts of government begets mildness and moderation, by instructing men in the advantages of human maxims above rigour and severity, which drive subjects into rebellion, and make the return to submission impracticable, by cutting off all hopes of pardon. When the tempers of men are softened as well as their knowledge improved, this humanity appears still more conspicuous, and is the chief characteristic which distinguishes a civilized age from times of barbarity and ignorance. Factions are then less inveterate, revolutions less tragical, authority less severe and seditions less frequent. Even foreign wars abate of their cruelty; and after the field of battle where honour and interest steel men against compassion, as well as fear, the combatants divest themselves of the brute, and resume the man.

Nor need we fear, that men, by losing their ferocity, will lose their martial spirit, or become less undaunted and vigorous in defense of their country or their liberty. The arts have no such effect in enervating either the mind or body. On the contrary, industry, their inseparable attendant, adds new force to both. And if anger which is said to be the whetstone of courage, loses somewhat of its asperity, by politeness and refinement; a sense of honour, which is a stronger, more constant and more governable principle, acquires fresh vigour by that elevation of genius which arises from knowledge and a good education. Add to this that courage can neither have any duration, nor be of any use, when not accompanied with discipline and martial skill, which are seldom found among a barbarous people. The ancients remarked, that Datames was the only barbarian that ever knew the art of war. And Pyrrhus, seeing the Romans marshal their army with some art and skill said with surprise, *These barbarians have nothing barbarous in their discipline!* It is observable, that, as the old Romans, by applying themselves solely to war were almost the only uncivilized people that ever possessed military discipline; so the modern Italians are the only civilized people, among Europeans, that ever wanted courage and a martial spirit. Those who would ascribe this effeminacy of the Italians to their luxury, or politeness, or application to the arts, need but consider the French and English, whose bravery is as incontestable as their love for the arts, and their assiduity in commerce. The Italian historians give us a more satisfactory reason for the degeneracy of their countrymen. They show us how the sword was dropped at once by all the Italian sovereigns; while the Venetian aristocracy was jealous of its subjects, the Florentine democracy applied itself entirely to commerce; Rome was governed by priests, and Naples by women. War then became the business of soldiers of fortune, who spared one another, and, to the astonishment of the world, could engage a whole day in what they called a battle, and return at night to their camp without the least bloodshed.

What has chiefly induced severe moralists to declaim against refinement in the arts, is the example of ancient Rome, which, joining to its poverty and rusticity virtue and public spirit, rose to such a surprising height of grandeur and liberty; but, having learned from its conquered provinces the Asiatic luxury, fell into every kind of corruption; whence arose sedition and civil wars, attended at last with the total loss of liberty. All the Latin classics, whom we peruse in our infancy, are full of these sentiments, and universally ascribe the ruin of their state to the arts and riches imported from the East; insomuch, that Sallust represents a taste for painting as a vice, no less than lewdness and drinking. And so popular were these sentiments, during the latter ages of the republic, that this author abounds in praises of the old rigid Roman virtue, though himself the most egregious instance of modern luxury and corruption; speaks contemptuously of the Grecian eloquence, though the most elegant writer in the world; nay, employs preposterous digressions and declamations to this purpose, though a model of taste and correctness.

But it would be easy to prove, that these writers mistook the cause of the disorders in the Roman state, and ascribed to luxury and the arts, what really proceeded from an ill-modeled government, and the unlimited extent of conquests. Refinement on the pleasures and conveniences of life has no natural tendency to beget venality and corruption. The value which all men put upon any particular pleasure, depends on comparison and experience; nor is a porter less greedy of money, which he spends on bacon and brandy, than a courtier, who purchases champagne and ortolans. Riches are valuable at all times, and to all men; because they always purchase pleasures, such as men are accustomed to and desire: nor can any thing restrain or regulate the love of money, but a sense of honour and virtue; which, if it be not nearly equal at all times, will naturally abound most in ages of knowledge and refinement.

Of all European kingdoms Poland seems the most defective in the arts of war as well as peace, mechanical as well as liberal; yet it is there that venality and corruption do most prevail. The nobles seem to have preserved their crown elective for no other purpose, than regularly to sell it to the highest bidder. This is almost the only species of commerce with which that people are acquainted.

The liberties of England, so far from decaying since the improvements in the arts, have never flourished so much as during that period. And though corruption may seem to increase of late years; this is chiefly to be ascribed to our established liberty, when our princes have found the impossibility of governing without parliaments, or of terrifying parliaments by the phantom of prerogative. Not to mention, that this corruption or venality prevails much more among the electors than the elected; and therefore cannot justly be ascribed to any refinements in luxury.

If we consider the matter in a proper light, we shall find, that a progress in the arts is rather favourable to liberty, and has a natural tendency to preserve, if not produce a free government. In rude unpolished nations, where the arts are neglected, all labour is bestowed on the cultivation of the ground; and the whole society is divided into two classes, proprietors of land, and their vassals or tenants. The latter are necessarily dependent, and fitted for slavery and subjection; especially where they possess no riches, and are not valued for their knowledge in agriculture; as must always be the case where the arts are neglected. The former naturally erect themselves into petty tyrants; and must either submit to an absolute master, for the sake of peace and order; or, if they will preserve their independency, like the ancient barons, they must fall into feuds and contests among themselves, and throw the whole society into such confusion, as is perhaps worse than the most despotic government. But where luxury nourishes commerce and industry, the peasants, by a proper cultivation of the land become rich and independent: while the tradesmen and merchants acquire a share of the property, and draw authority and consideration to that middling rank of men, who are the best and firmest basis of public liberty. These submit not to slavery like the peasants, from poverty and meanness of spirit; and, having no hopes of tyrannizing over others, like the barons, they are not tempted, for the sake of that gratification, to submit to the tyranny of their sovereign. They covet equal laws, which may secure their property, and preserve them from monarchical, as well as aristocratic tyranny.

The lower house is the support of our popular government; and all the world acknowledges, that it owed its chief influence and consideration to the increase of commerce, which threw such a balance of property into the hands of the Commons. How inconsistent, then, is it to blame so violently a refinement in the arts, and to represent it as the bane of liberty and public spirit!

To declaim against present times, and magnify the virtue of remote ancestors, is a propensity almost inherent in human nature: and as the sentiments and opinions of civilized ages alone are transmitted to posterity, hence it is that we meet with so many severe judgments pronounced against luxury, and even science; and hence it is that at present we give so ready an assent to them. But the fallacy is easily perceived, by comparing different nations that are contemporaries; where we both judge more impartially, and can better set in opposition those manners, with which we are sufficiently acquainted. Treachery and cruelty, the most pernicious and most odious of all vices, seem peculiar to uncivilized ages; and, by the refined Greeks and Romans, were ascribed to all the barbarous nations which surrounded them. They might justly, therefore, have presumed, that their own ancestors, so highly celebrated, possessed no greater virtue, and were as much inferior to their posterity in honour and humanity, as in taste and science. An ancient Frank or Saxon may be highly extolled: but I believe every man would think his life or fortune much less secure in the hands of a Moor or Tartar, than in those of a French or English gentleman, the rank of men the most civilized in the most civilized nations.

We come now to the second position which we proposed to illustrate, to wit, that, as innocent luxury, or a refinement in the arts and conveniences of life, is advantageous to the public; so, wherever luxury ceases to be innocent, it also ceases to be beneficial; and when carried a degree further, begins to be a quality pernicious, though perhaps not the most pernicious, to political society.

Let us consider what we call vicious luxury. No gratification, however sensual, can of itself be esteemed vicious. A gratification is only vicious when it engrosses all a man's expense, and leaves no ability for such acts of duty and generosity as are required by his situation and fortune. Suppose that he correct the vice, and employ part of his expense in the education of his children, in the support of his friends, and in relieving the poor; would any prejudice result to society? On the contrary, the same consumption would arise; and that labour, which at present is employed only in producing a slender gratification to one man, would relieve the necessitous, and bestow satisfaction on hundreds. The same care and toil that raise a dish of peas at Christmas, would give bread to a whole family, during six months. To say that without a vicious luxury, the labour would not have been employed at all, is only to say, that there is some other defect in human nature, such as indolence, selfishness, inattention to others, for which luxury, in some measure, provides a remedy; as one poison may be an antidote to another. But virtue, like wholesome food, is better than poisons, however corrected.

Suppose the same number of men that are at present in Great Britain, with the same soil and climate; I ask, is it not possible for them to be happier, by the most perfect way of life that can be imagined, and by the greatest reformation that Omnipotence itself could work in their temper and disposition? To assert that they cannot, appears evidently ridiculous. As the land is able to maintain more than all its present inhabitants they would never in such a Utopian state, feel any other ills than those which arise from bodily sickness: and these are not the half of human miseries. All other ills spring from some vice, either in ourselves or others; and even many of our diseases proceed from the same origin. Remove the vices, and the ills follow. You must only take care to remove all the vices. If you remove part, you may render the matter worse. By banishing *vicious* luxury, without curing sloth and an indifference to others, you only diminish industry in the state, and add nothing to men's charity or their generosity. Let us, therefore, rest contented with asserting, that two opposite vices in a state may be more advantageous than either of them alone; but let us never pronounce vice in itself advantageous. It is not very inconsistent for an author to assert in one page, that moral distinctions are inventions of politicians for public interest, and in the next page maintain, that vice is advantageous to the public. And indeed it seems, upon any system of morality, little less than a contradiction in terms, to talk of a vice, which is in general beneficial to society.

I thought this reasoning necessary, in order to give some light to a philosophical question, which has been much disputed in England. I call it a *philosophical* question, not a *political* one. For whatever may be the consequence of such a miraculous transformation of mankind, as would endow them with every species of virtue, and free them from every species of vice, this concerns not the magistrate, who aims only at possibilities. He cannot cure every vice by substituting a virtue in its place. Very often he can only cure one vice by another; and in that case he ought to prefer what is least pernicious to society. Luxury, when excessive, is the source of many ills, but is in general preferable to sloth and idleness, which would commonly succeed in its place, and are more hurtful both to private persons and to the public. When sloth reigns, a mean uncultivated way of life prevails amongst individuals, without society, without enjoyment. And if the sovereign, in such a situation, demands the service of his subjects, the labour of the state suffices only to furnish the necessaries of life to the labourers, and can afford nothing to those who are employed in the public service.

Two

Adam Smith
(1723–1790)

LECTURES ON JURISPUDENCE (1766)

Part II: Of Police

Police is the second general division of jurisprudence. The name is French, and is originally derived from the Greek *politeia*, which properly signified the policy of civil government, but now it only means the regulation of the inferiour parts of government, viz. cleanliness, security, and cheapness or plenty. The two former, to wit, the proper method of carrying dirt from the streets, and the execution of justice, so far as it regards regulations for preventing crimes or the method of keeping a city guard, though useful, are too mean to be considered in a general discourse of this kind. An observation or two before we proceed to the third particular is all that is necessary.

We observe then, that in cities where there is most police and the greatest number of regulations concerning it, there is not always the greatest security. In Paris the regulations concerning police are so numerous as not to be comprehended in several volumes. In London there are only two or three simple regulations. Yet in Paris scarce a night passes without somebody being killed, while in London, which is a larger city, there are scarce three or four in a year. On this account one would be apt to think that the more police there is the less security, but this is not the cause. In England as well as in France, during the time of the feudal government and as late as Queen Elizabeth's reign, great numbers of retainers were kept idle about the noblemen's houses, to keep the tenants in awe. These retainers, when turned out, had no other way of getting their subsistence but by committing robberies and living on plunder, which occasioned the greatest disorder. A remain of the feudal manners, still preserved in France, gives occasion to the difference. The nobility at Paris keep far more menial servants than ours, who are often turned out on their own account or through the caprice of their masters, and, being in the most indigent circumstances, are forced to commit the most dreadful crimes. In Glasgow, where almost no body has more than one servant, there are fewer capital crimes than in Edinburgh. In Glasgow there is not one in several years, but not a year passes in Edinburgh without some such disorders. Upon this principle, therefore, it is not so much the police that prevents the commission of crimes as the having as few persons as possible to live upon others. Nothing tends so much to corrupt mankind as dependency, while independency still increases the honesty of the people. The establishment of commerce and manufactures, which brings about this independency, is the best police for preventing crimes. The common people have better wages in this way than in any other, and in consequence of this a general probity of manners takes place through the whole country. No body will be so mad as to expose himself upon the highway, when he can make better bread in an honest and industrious manner. The nobility of Paris and London are no doubt much upon a level, but the common people of the former, being much more dependent, are not to be compared with these of the latter, and for the same reason the commonality in Scotland differ from these in England, though the nobility too are much upon a level.

Thus far for the two first particulars which come under the general division of police. In the following part of this discourse we are to confine ourselves to the consideration of cheapness or plenty, or, which is the same thing, the most proper way of procuring wealth and abundance.

...

In an uncivilized nation, and where labour is undivided, every thing is provided for that the natural wants of mankind require; yet when the nation is cultivated and labour divided a more liberal provision is allotted them; and it is on this account that a common day labourer in Britain has more luxury in his way of living than an Indian sovereign. The woolen coat he wears requires very considerable preparations; the wool gatherer, the dresser, the spinster, the dyer, the weaver, the tailor, and many more must all be employed before the labourer is clothed. The tools by which all this is effectuated employ a still greater number of artists, the loom maker, mill wright, ropemaker, not to mention the bricklayer, the treefeller, the miner, the smelter, the forger, the smith, etc. Besides his dress, consider also his household furniture, his coarse linens, his shoes, his coals dug out of the earth or brought by sea, his kitchen utensils and different plates, those that are employed in providing his bread and beer, the sower, the brewer, the reaper, the baker, his glass windows and the art required in preparing them, without which our northern climate could hardly be inhabited. When we examine the conveniences of the day labourer, we find that even in his easy simple manner he cannot be accommodated without the assistance of a great number, and yet this is nothing compared with the luxury of the nobility. An European prince, however, does not so far exceed a commoner as the latter does the chief of a savage nation. It is easy to conceive how the rich can be so well provided for, as they can direct so many hands to serve their purposes. They are supported by the industry of the peasant. In a savage nation every one enjoys the whole fruit of his own labour, yet their indigence is greater than any where.

It is the division of labour which increases the opulence of a country. In a civilized society, though there is indeed a division of labour there is no equal division, for there are a good many who work none at all. The division of opulence is not according to the work. The opulence of the merchant is greater than that of all his clerks, though he works less; and they again have six times more than an equal number of artisans, who are more employed. The artisan who works at his ease within doors has far more than the poor labourer who trudges up and down without intermission. Thus he who, as it were, bears the burden of society has the fewest advantages.

We shall next show how this division of labour occasions a multiplication of the product, or, which is the same thing, how opulence arises from it. In order to this let us observe the effect of the division of labour in some manufactures. If all the parts of a pin were made by one man, if the same person dug the ore, smelted it, and split the wire, it would take him a whole year to make one pin, and this pin must therefore be sold at the expense of his maintenance for that time, which taking it at a moderate computation would at least be six pounds for a pin. If the labour is so far divided that the wire is ready made, he will not make above 20 per day, which allowing 10 pence for wages makes the pin twopence. The pin maker therefore divides the labour among a great number of different persons, the cutting, pointing, heading, and gilding are all separate professions. Two or three are employed in making the head, one or two in putting it on, and so on, to the putting them in the paper, being in all eighteen. By this division every one can with great ease make 2000 a day. The same is the case in the linen and woolen manufactures. Some arts, however, there are which will not admit of this division, and therefore they cannot keep pace with other manufactures and arts. Such are farming and grazing. This is entirely owing to the returns of the seasons, by which one man can only be for a short time employed in any one operation. In countries where the seasons do not make such alterations it is otherwise. In France the corn is better and cheaper than in England. But our toys, which have no dependence on the climate and in which labour can be divided, are far superiour to those of France.

When labour is thus divided, and so much done by one man in proportion, the surplus above their maintenance is considerable, which each man can exchange for a fourth of what he could have done if he had finished it alone. By this means the commodity becomes far cheaper, and the labour dearer. It is to be observed that the price of labour by no means determines the opulence of society. It is only when a little labour can procure abundance. On this account a rich nation, when its manufactures are greatly improved, may have an advantage over a poor one by underselling it. The cotton and other commodities from China would undersell any made with us, were it not for the long carriage and other taxes that are laid upon them.

We must not judge of the dearness of labour by the money or coin that is paid for it. One penny in some places will purchase as much as eighteenpence in others. In the country of the Mogul, where the days wages are only twopence, labour is better rewarded than in some of our sugar islands, where men are almost starving with four or five shillings a day. Coin therefore can be no proper estimate. Further, though human labour be employed both in the multiplication of commodities and of money, yet the chance of success is not equal. A farmer by the proper cultivation of an acre is sure of increase, but the miner may work again and again without success. Commodities must therefore multiply in greater proportion than gold and silver.

But again, the quantity of work which is done by the division of labour is much increased by the three following articles, first, increase of dexterity, secondly, the saving of time lost in passing from one species of labour to another, and thirdly, the invention of machinery.

We have already shown that the division of labour is the immediate cause of opulence. We shall next consider what gives occasion to the division of labour, or from what principles in our nature it can best be accounted for. We cannot imagine this to be an effect of human prudence. It was indeed made a law by Sesostratis that every man should follow the employment of his father. But this is by no means suitable to the dispositions of human nature and can never long take place. Every one is fond of being a gentleman, be his father what he would. They who are strongest and in the bustle of society have got above the weak, must have as many under as to defend them in their station; from necessary causes, therefore, there must be as many in the lower stations as there is occasion for. There must be as many up as down, and no division can be overstretched. But it is not this which gives occasion to the division of labour. It flows from a direct propensity in human nature for one man to barter with another, which is common to all men and known to no other animal. No body ever saw a dog, the most sagacious animal, exchange a bone with his companion for another. Two greyhounds, indeed, in running down a hare, seem to have something like compact or agreement betwixt them, but this is nothing else but a concurrence of the same passions. If an animal intends to truck, as it were, or gain any thing from man, it is by its fondness and kindness. Man, in the same manner, works on the self-love of his fellows, by setting before them a sufficient temptation to get what he wants; the language of this disposition is, give me what I want, and you shall have what you want. It is not from benevolence, as the dogs, but from self-love that man expects any thing. The brewer and the baker serve us not from benevolence but from self-love. No man but a beggar depends on benevolence, and even they would die in a week were their entire dependence upon it.

By this disposition to barter and exchange the surplus of one's labour for that of other people, in a nation of hunters, if any one has a talent for making bows and arrows better than his neighbours he will at first make presents of them, and in return get presents of their game. By continuing this practice he will live better than before and will have no occasion to provide for himself, as the surplus of his own labour does it more effectually.

This disposition to barter is by no means founded upon different genius and talents. It is doubtful if there be any such difference at all; at least it is far less than we are aware of. Genius is more the effect of the division of labour than the latter is of it. The difference between a porter and a philosopher in the first four or five years of their life is properly speaking none at all. When they come to be employed in different occupations, their views widen and differ by degrees. As every one has this natural disposition to truck and barter by which he provides for himself, there is no need for such different endowments, and accordingly among savages there is always the greatest uniformity of character. In other animals of the same species we find a much greater difference than betwixt the philosopher and porter antecedent to custom. The mastiff and spaniel have quite different powers, but though these animals are possessed of talents they cannot, as it were, bring them into the common stock and exchange their productions, and therefore their different talents are of no use to them.

It is quite otherwise among mankind; they can exchange their several productions according to their quantity or quality. The philosopher and the porter are both of advantage to each other. The porter is of use in carrying burdens for the philosopher, and in his turn he burns his coals cheaper by the philosopher's invention of the fire machine. Thus we have shown that different genius is not the foundation of this disposition to barter, which is the cause of the division of labour. The real foundation of it is that principle to persuade which so much prevails in human nature. When any arguments are offered to persuade, it is always expected that they should have their proper effect. If a person asserts any thing about the moon, though it should not be true, he will feel a kind of uneasiness in being contradicted, and would be very glad that the person he is endeavouring to persuade should be of the same way of thinking with himself. We ought then mainly to cultivate the power of persuasion, and indeed we do so without intending it. Since a whole life is spent in the exercise of it, a ready method of bargaining with each other must undoubtedly be attained. As was before observed, no animal can do this but by gaining the favour of those whom they would persuade. Sometimes, indeed, animals seem to act in concert, but there never is any thing like bargain among them. Monkeys when they rob a garden throw the fruit from one to another till they deposit it in the hoard, but there is always a scramble about the division of the booty, and usually some of them are killed.

From all that has been said we may observe that the division of labour must always be proportioned to the extent of commerce. If ten people only want a certain commodity, the manufacture of it will never be so divided as if a thousand wanted it. Again, the division of labour, in order to opulence, becomes always more perfect by the easy method of conveyance in a country. If the road be infested with robbers, if it be deep and conveyance not easy, the progress of commerce must be stopped. Since the mending of roads in England 40 or 50 years ago, its opulence has increased extremely. Water carriage is another convenience, as by it 300 ton can be conveyed at the expense of the tare and wear of the vessel and the wages of 5 or 6 men, and that too in a shorter time than by 100 wagons, which will take 6 horses and a man each. Thus the division of labour is the great cause of the increase of public opulence, which is always proportioned to the industry of the people, and not to the quantity of gold and silver as is foolishly imagined, and the industry of the people is always proportioned to the division of labour.

Having thus shown what gives occasion to public opulence, in farther considering this subject we propose to consider:
1st. What circumstances regulate the price of commodities.
2dly. Money in two different views, first as the measure of value and then as the instrument of commerce.
3dly. The history of commerce, in which shall be taken notice of the causes of the slow progress of opulence both in ancient and modern times, which causes shall be shown either to affect agriculture or arts and manufactures. Lastly, the effects of a commercial spirit on the government, temper, and manners of a people, whether good or bad, and the proper remedies. Of these in order.

Of every commodity there are two different prices, which though apparently independent will be found to have a necessary connection, viz. the natural price and the market price. Both of these are regulated by certain circumstances. When men are induced to a certain species of industry rather than any other, they must make as much by the employment as will maintain them while they are employed. An arrow maker must be sure to exchange as much surplus product as will maintain him during as long time as he took to make them. But upon this principle in the different trades there must be a considerable difference, because some trades, such as these of the tailor and weaver, are not learned by casual observation and a little experience, like that of the day-labourer, but take a great deal of time and pains before they are acquired. When a person begins them, for a considerable time his work is of no use to his master or any other person, and therefore his master must be compensated both for what maintains him and for what he spoils. When he comes to exercise his trade, he must be repaid what he has laid out, both of expenses and of apprentice fee. And as his life is not worth above 10 or 12 years purchase at most, his wages must be high on account of the risk he runs of not having the whole made up. But again, there are many arts which require more extensive knowledge than is to be got during the time of an apprenticeship. A blacksmith and weaver may learn their business well enough without any previous knowledge of mathematics. But a watch maker must be acquainted with several sciences in order to understand his business well, such as arithmetic, geometry, and astronomy with regard to the equation of time, and their wages must be high in order to compensate the additional expense. In general, this is the case in all the liberal arts, because after they have spent a long time in their education it is ten to one if ever they make any thing by it. Their wages therefore must be higher in proportion to the expense they have been at, the risk of not living long enough, and the risk of not having dexterity enough to manage their business. Among the lawyers there is not one among twenty that attains such knowledge and dexterity in his business as enables him to get back the expenses of his education, and many of them never make the price of their gown, as we say. The fees of lawyers are so far from being extravagant, as they are generally thought, that they are rather low in proportion. It is the eminence of the profession, and not the money made by it, that is the temptation for applying to it, and the dignity of that rank is to be considered as a part of what is made by it.

In the same manner we shall find that the price of gold and silver is not extravagant if we consider it in this view, for in a gold or silver mine there is a great chance of missing it altogether. If we suppose an equal number of men employed in raising corn and digging silver, the former will make more than the latter, because perhaps of forty or fifty employed in a mine only twenty make any thing at all. Some of the rest may indeed make fortunes, but every cornman succeeds in his undertakings, so that upon the whole there is more made this way than the other. It is the ideal acquisition which is the principal temptation in a mine. A man then has the natural price of his labour when it is sufficient to maintain him during the time of labour, to defray the expense of education, and to compensate the risk of not living long enough and of not succeeding in the business. When a man has this, there is sufficient encouragement to the labourer and the commodity will be cultivated in proportion to the demand.

The market price of goods is regulated by quite other circumstances. When a buyer comes to the market, he never asks of the seller what expenses he has been at in producing them. The regulation of the market price of goods depends on the three following articles:

1st. The demand or need for the commodity. There is no demand for a thing of little use; it is not a rational object of desire.

2dly. The abundance or scarcity of the commodity in proportion to the need of it. If the commodity be scarce, the price is raised, but if the quantity be more than is sufficient to supply the demand, the price falls. Thus it is that diamonds and other precious stones are dear, while iron, which is much more useful, is so many times cheaper, though this depends principally on the last cause, viz.

3dly. The riches or poverty of those who demand. When there is not enough produced to serve every body, the fortune of the bidders is the only regulation of the price.

The story which is told of the merchant and the carrier in the deserts of Arabia is an evidence of this. The merchant gave 10,000 ducats for a certain quantity of water. His fortune here regulated the price, for if he had not had them, he could not have given them, and if his fortune had been less, the water would have been cheaper. When the commodity is scarce, the seller must be content with that degree of wealth which they have who buy it. The case is much the same as in an auction; if two persons have an equal fondness for a book, he whose fortune is largest will carry it. Hence things that are very rare go always to rich countries. The King of France only could purchase that large diamond of so many thousand pounds value. Upon this principle every thing is dearer or cheaper according as it is the purchase of a higher or lower set of people.

Utensils of gold are comeatable only by persons in certain circumstances. These of silver fall to another set of people and their prices are regulated by what the majority can give. The prices of corn and beer are regulated by what all the world can give, and on this account the wages of the day-labourer have a great influence upon the price of corn. When the price of corn rises, wages rise also, and vice versa. When the quantity of corn falls short, as in a sea voyage, it always occasions a famine and then the price becomes enormous. Corn then becomes the purchase of a higher set of people, and the lower must live on turnips and potatoes.

Thus we have considered the two prices, the natural and the market price, which every commodity is supposed to have. We observed before that however seemingly independent they appear to be, they are necessarily connected. This will appear from the following considerations. If the market price of any commodity is very great, and the labour very highly rewarded, the market is prodigiously crowded with it, greater quantities of it are produced, and it can be sold to the inferiour ranks of people. If for every ten diamonds there were ten thousand, they would become the purchase of every body, because they would become very cheap, and would sink to their natural price. Again, when the market is overstocked and there is not enough got for the labour of the manufacture, no body will bind to it; they cannot have a subsistence by it, because the market price falls then below the natural price. It is alleged that as the price of corn sinks, the wages of the labourer should sink, as he is then better rewarded. It is true that if provisions were long cheap, as more people would flock to this labour where the wages are high, through this concurrence of labour the wages would come down. But we find that when the price of corn is doubled the wages continue the same as before, because the labourers have no other way to turn themselves. The same is the case with menial servants.

From the above we may observe that whatever police tends to raise the market price above the natural, tends to diminish public opulence. Dearness and scarcity are in effect the same thing. When commodities are in abundance, they can be sold to the inferiour ranks of people, who can afford to give less for them, but not if they are scarce. So far therefore as goods are a convenience to the society, the society lives less happy when only the few can possess them. Whatever therefore keeps goods above their natural price for a permanence, diminishes a nations opulence. Such are:

1st. All taxes upon industry, upon leather, and upon shoes, which people grudge most, upon salt, beer, or whatever is the strong drink of the country, for no country wants some kind of it. Man is an anxious animal and must have his care swept off by something that can exhilarate the spirits. It is alleged that this tax upon beer is an artificial security against drunkenness, but if we attend to it, we shall find that it by no means prevents it. In countries where strong liquors are cheap, as in France and Spain, the people are generally sober. But in northern countries, where they are dear, they do not get drunk with beer but with spirituous liquors. No body presses his friend to a glass of beer unless he choose it.

2dly. Monopolies also destroy public opulence. The price of the monopolized goods is raised above what is sufficient for encouraging the labour. When only a certain person or persons have the liberty of importing a commodity, there is less of it imported than would otherwise be: the price of it is therefore higher, and fewer people supported by it. It is the concurrence of different labourers which always brings down the price. In monopolies such as the Hudson's Bay and East India companies the people engaged in them make the price what they please.

3dly. Exclusive privileges of corporations have the same effect. The butchers and bakers raise the price of their goods as they please, because none but their own corporation is allowed to sell in the market, and therefore their meat must be taken, whether good or not. On this account there is always required a magistrate to fix the prices. For any free commodity, such as broad cloth, there is no occasion for this, but it is necessary with bakers, who may agree among themselves to make the quantity and price what they please. Even a magistrate is not a good enough expedient for this, as he must always settle the price at the outside, else the remedy must be worse than the disease, for no body would apply to these businesses and a famine would ensue. On this account bakers and brewers have always profitable trades.

As what rises the market price above the natural one diminishes public opulence, so what brings it down below it has the same effect.

It is only upon manufactures to be exported that this can usually be done by any law or regulation, such as the bounty allowed by the government upon coarse linen, by which it becomes exportable when under 12 pence a yard. The public paying a great part of the price, it can be sold cheaper to foreigners than what is sufficient for encouraging the labour. In the same manner, by the bounty of five shillings upon the quarter of corn when sold under 40 shillings, as the public pays an eight part of the price, it can be sold just so much cheaper at a foreign market. By this bounty the commodity is rendered more comeatable, and a greater quantity of it produced, but then it breaks what may be called the natural balance of industry. The disposition to apply to the production of that commodity is not proportioned to the natural cause of the demand, but to both that and the annexed bounty. But it has not only this effect with regard to the particular commodity, but likewise people are called from other productions which are less encouraged, and thus the balance of industry is broken.

Again, after the ages of hunting and fishing, in which provisions were the immediate produce of their labour, when manufactures were introduced, nothing could be produced without a great deal of time. It was a long time before the weaver could carry to the market the cloth which he bought in flax. Every trade therefore requires a stock of food, clothes, and lodging to carry it on.

Suppose then, as is really the case in every country, that there is in store a stock of food, clothes, and lodging, the number of people that are employed must be in proportion to it. If the price of one commodity is sunk below its natural price, while another is above it, there is a smaller quantity of the stored stock left to support the whole, on account of the natural connection of all trades in the stock. By allowing bounties to me you take away the stock from the rest. This has been the real consequence of the corn bounty.

The price of corn being sunk, the rent of the farms sinks also, yet the bounty upon corn, which was laid on at the time of the taxes, was intended to raise the rent, and had the effect for sometime, because the tenants were assured of a price for their corn both at home and abroad. But though the effects of the bounty encouraging agriculture brought down the price of corn, yet it raised the grass-farms, for the more corn the less grass.

The price of grass being raised, butcher's meat, in consequence of its dependence upon it, must be raised also. So that if the price of corn is diminished, the price of other commodities is necessarily raised. The price of corn has indeed fallen from 42 to 35, but the price of hay has risen from 25 to near 50 shillings. As the price of hay has risen, horses are not so easily kept, and therefore the price of carriage has risen also. But whatever increases the price of carriage diminishes plenty in the market. Upon the whole, therefore, it is by far the best police to leave things to their natural course, and allow no bounties, nor impose taxes on commodities. Thus we have shown what circumstances regulate the price of commodities, which was the first thing proposed.

We come now to the second particular, to consider money, first as the measure of value and then as the medium of permutation or exchange.

When people deal in many species of goods, one of them must be considered as the measure of value. Suppose there were only three commodities, sheep, corn, and oxen, we can easily remember them comparatively. But if we have a hundred different commodities, there are ninety nine values of each arising from a comparison with each of the rest. As these cannot easily be remembered, men naturally fall upon one of them to be a common standard with which they compare all the rest. This will naturally at first be the commodity with which they are best acquainted. Accordingly we find that black cattle and sheep were the standard in Homer's time. The armour of one of his heroes was worth nine oxen, and that of another worth an hundred. Black cattle was the common standard in ancient Greece. In Italy, and particularly in Tuscany, every thing was compared with sheep, as this was their principal commodity. This is what may be called the natural measure of value.

In like manner there were natural measures of quantity, such as fathoms, cubits, inches, taken from the proportions of the human body, once in use with every nation. But by a little observation they found that one man's arm was longer or shorter than another's, and that one was not to be compared with the other, and therefore wise men who attended to these things would endeavour to fix upon some more accurate measure, that equal quantities might be of equal values. This method became absolutely necessary when people came to deal in many commodities and in great quantities of them. Though an inch was altogether inconsiderable when their dealings were confined to a few yards, more accuracy was required when they came to deal in some thousands. We find, in countries where their dealings are small, the remains of this inaccuracy. The cast of the balance is nothing thought of in their coarse commodities.

Since, then, there must of necessity be a common standard of which equal quantities should be of equal values, metals in general seemed best to answer this purpose, and of these the value of gold and silver could best be ascertained. The temper of steel cannot be precisely known, but what degree of alloy is in gold and silver can be exactly found out. Gold and silver were therefore fixed upon as the most exact standard to compare goods with, and were therefore considered as the most proper measure of value.

In consequence of gold and silver becoming the measure of value, it came also to be the instrument of commerce. It soon became necessary that goods should be carried to market, and they could never be cleverly exchanged unless the measure of value was also the instrument of commerce. In the age of shepherds it might be no great inconvenience that cattle should be the medium of exchange, as the expense of maintaining them was nothing, the whole country being considered as one great common. But when lands came to be divided and the division of labour introduced, this custom would be productive of very considerable inconveniences. The butcher and shoemaker might at times have no use for one another's commodities. The farmer very often cannot maintain upon his ground a cow more than he has; it would be a very great hardship on a Glasgow merchant to give him a cow for one of his commodities. To remedy this, these materials which were before considered as the measure of value came also to be the instrument of exchange. Gold and silver had all advantages; they can be kept without expense, they do not waste, and they are very portable. Gold and silver however do not derive their whole utility from being the medium of exchange. Though they never had been used as money, they are more valuable than any other metals. They have a superior beauty, are capable of a finer polish, and are more proper for making any instrument except these with an edge. For all these reasons gold and silver came to be the proper measure of value and the instrument of exchange. But in order to render them more proper for these purposes, it was necessary that both their weight and their fineness should be ascertained. At first their balances were not very accurate and therefore frauds were easily committed; however, this was remedied by degrees.

But common business would not allow of the experiments which are necessary to fix precisely the degree of fineness; though with a great quantity of alloy, they are to appearance good. It was necessary therefore, to facilitate exchange, that they should fall upon some expedient to ascertain with accuracy both weight and fineness. Coinage most effectually secures both these. The public, finding how much it would tend to facilitate commerce, put a stamp upon certain pieces, that whoever saw them might have the public faith that they were of a certain weight and fineness; and this would be what was at first marked upon the coin, as being of most importance.

Accordingly the coins of every country appear to have been the names of the weights corresponding to them, and they contained the denomination they expressed. The British pound sterling seems originally to have been a pound weight of pure silver. As gold could be easily exchanged into silver, the latter came always to be the standard or measure of value. As there cannot be two standards, and in the greater part of purchases silver is necessary, we never say a man is worth so many guineas, but always pounds…

We have shown what rendered money the measure of value, but it is to be observed that labour, not money, is the true measure of value. National opulence consists therefore in the quantity of goods and the facility of barter. This shall next be considered.

The more money that is necessary to circulate the goods of any country, the more is the quantity of goods diminished. Suppose that the whole stock of Scotland in corn, cattle, money, etc. amounts to 20 millions, and if one million in cash is necessary to carry on the circulation, there will be in the country only 19 millions of food, clothes, and lodging, and the people have less by one million than they would have if there were no occasion for this expedient of money. It is therefore evident that the poverty of any country increases as the money increases, money being a dead stock in itself, supplying no convenience of life. Money in this respect may be compared to the high roads of a country, which bear neither corn nor grass themselves but circulate all the corn and grass in the country. If we could find any way to save the ground taken up by highways, we would increase considerably the quantity of commodities and have more to carry to the market. In the same manner as the value of a piece of ground does not lie in the number of highways that run through it, so the riches of a country does not consist in the quantity of money employed to circulate commerce, but in the great abundance of the necessaries of life. If we could therefore fall on a method to send the half of our money abroad to be converted into goods, and at the same time supply the channel of circulation at home, we would greatly increase the wealth of the country...

We come now to the next thing proposed, to examine the causes of the slow progress of opulence.

When one considers the effects of the division of labour, what an immediate tendency it has to improve the arts, it appears somewhat surprising that every nation should continue so long in a poor and indigent state as we find it does. The causes of this may be considered under these two heads, first, natural impediments, and secondly, the oppression of civil government.

A rude and barbarous people are ignorant of the effects of the division of labour, and it is long before one person, by continually working at different things, can produce any more than is necessary for his daily subsistence. Before labour can be divided some accumulation of stock is necessary. A poor man with no stock can never begin a manufacture. Before a man can commence farmer he must at least have laid in a years' provision, because he does not receive the fruits of his labour till the end of the season. Agreeably to this, in a nation of hunters or shepherds no person can quit the common trade in which he is employed, and which affords him daily subsistence, till he have some stock to maintain him and begin the new trade. Every one knows how difficult it is, even in a refined society, to raise one's self to moderate circumstances. It is still more difficult to raise one's self by these trades which require no art nor ingenuity. A porter or day labourer must continue poor for ever. In the beginnings of society this is still more difficult. Bare subsistence is almost all that a savage can procure, and having no stock to begin upon, nothing to maintain him but what is produced by the exertion of his own strength, it is no wonder that he continues long in an indigent state. The meanest labourer in a polished society has in many respects an advantage over a savage. He has more assistance in his labour; he has only one particular thing to do, which by assiduity he attains a facility in performing; he has also machines and instruments which greatly assist him. An Indian has not so much as a pick-ax, a spade, or a shovel, nor any thing else but his own labour. This is one great cause of the slow progress of opulence in every country; till some stock be produced there can be no division of labour, and before a division of labour take place there can be very little accumulation of stock.

The other cause that was assigned was the nature of civil government. In the infancy of society, as has been often observed, government must be weak and feeble, and it is long before its authority can protect the industry of individuals from the rapacity of their neighbours. When people find themselves every moment in danger of being robbed of all they possess, they have no motive to be industrious. There could be little accumulation of stock, because the indolent, which would be the greatest number, would live upon the industrious, and spend whatever they produced. When the power of government becomes so great as to defend the produce of industry, another obstacle arises from a different quarter. Among neighbouring nations in a barbarous state there are perpetual wars, one continually invading and plundering the other, and though private property be secured from the violence of neighbours, it is in danger from hostile invasions. In this manner it is next to impossible that any accumulation of stock can be made. It is observable that among savage nations there are always more violent convulsions than among those farther advanced in refinement. Among the Tartars and Arabs, great bands of barbarians are always roaming from one place to another in quest of plunder, and they pillage every country as they go along. Thus large tracts of country are often laid waste and all the effects carried away: Germany too was in the same condition about the fall of the Roman Empire. Nothing can be more an obstacle to the progress of opulence.

We shall next consider the effect of oppressive measures, first with regard to agriculture, and then with regard to commerce.

Agriculture is of all other arts the most beneficent to society, and whatever tends to retard its improvement is extremely prejudicial to the public interest. The produce of agriculture is much greater than that of any other manufacture. The rents of the whole lands in England amount to about 24 millions, and as the rent is generally about a third of the produce, the whole annual produce of the lands must be about 72 millions. This is much more than the produce of either the linen or woolen manufactures; for as the annual consumption is computed to be about 100 millions, if you deduce from this the 72 millions, the produce of agriculture, there will remain only 28 millions for all the other manufactures of the nation. Whatever measures, therefore, discourage the improvement of this art are extremely prejudicial to the progress of opulence.

One great hindrance to the progress of agriculture is the throwing great tracts of land into the hands of single persons. If any man's estate be more than he is able to cultivate, a part of it is in a manner lost. When a nation of savages takes possession of a country, the great and powerful divide the whole lands among them, and leave none for the lower ranks of people. In this manner the Celtae, and afterwards the Saxons, took possession of our own island.

When land is divided in great portions among the powerful, it is cultivated by slaves, which is a very unprofitable method of cultivation. The labour of a slave proceeds from no other motive but the dread of punishment, and if he could escape this he would work none at all. Should he exert himself in the most extraordinary manner, he cannot have the least expectations of any reward, and as all the produce of his labour goes to his master, he has no encouragement to industry. A young slave may perhaps exert himself a little at first, in order to attain his masters favour, but he soon finds that it is all in vain, and that, be his behaviour what it will, he will always meet with the same severe treatment. When lands, therefore, are cultivated by slaves, they cannot be greatly improved, as they have no motive to industry.

A cultivation of the same kind is that by villains. The landlord gave a man a piece of ground to cultivate, allowing him to maintain himself by it, and obliging him to restore whatever was over his own maintenance. This was equally unfavourable to the progress of agriculture, because the villains, who were a kind of slaves, had no motive to industry but their own maintenance. This objection lies equally against all cultivation by slaves. Some of the West India islands have indeed been cultivated by slaves, and have been greatly improved, but they might have been cultivated by freemen at less expense; and had not the profits of sugar been very great, the planters could not have supported the expense of slaves, but their profits have been so enormous that all the extraordinary expense of slave cultivation has vanished before it. In the northern colonies they employ few slaves, and though they are in a very flourishing condition in these colonies, the lands are generally cultivated by the proprietors, which is the most favourable method to the progress of agriculture. A tenant of the best kind has always a rent to pay, and therefore has much less to lay out on improvements. When a country sends out a colony, it may hinder a large tract of land to be occupied by a single person. But when savages take possession of a country, they are subject to no laws, the strongest man takes possession of most ground, and therefore among them agriculture cannot be quickly promoted.

After villains went out, as was explained before, tenants by steel bow succeeded. The landlord gave a farm with a stock to a villain, which were restored with half of the produce at the end of the year to the landlord. But as the tenant had no stock nor, though he had, any encouragement to lay it out on improvements, this method always was unfavourable to agriculture. For the same reason that tithes, by depriving the farmer of a tenth of his produce, hinder improvement, this, though in a higher degree, was a hindrance, because the tenant was deprived of one half of the produce. A great part of France is still cultivated by tenants of steel bow, and it is said that it still remains in some parts of the Highlands of Scotland.

The next species of cultivation was that by tenants, such as we have at present. Some of the tenants by steel bow, by extreme pinching and cunning, got a small stock laid up and offered their masters a fixed rent for the ground. Thus in progress of time the present method of cultivation was introduced, though it was long liable to inconveniences. If the landlord sold his land the new proprietor was not bound to the terms of agreement, and the tenant was often turned out of his farm. The landlord too invented a method to get rid of the tenant when he pleased by selling the estate to another, on whom he had a back bond to make him return the estate whenever the tenants were turned out. As the tenants were continually in danger of being turned out, they had no motive to improve the ground. This takes place to this day in every country of Europe except Britain. In Scotland contracts of this kind were rendered real rights in the reign of James III and in England in that of Henry VII.

Besides these there were several other impediments to the progress of agriculture. At first all rents were paid in kind, by which, in a dear year, the tenants were in danger of being ruined. A diminution of produce seldom hurts the tenant who pays his rent in money, because the price of corn rises in proportion to its scarcity. Society however is considerably advanced before money comes to be the whole instrument of commerce.

Another embarrassment was that the feudal lords sometimes allowed the king to levy subsidies from their tenants, which greatly discouraged their industry. Besides all, under the tyranny of the feudal aristocracy the landlords had nothing to stop them from squeezing their tenants and raising the rents of their lands as high as they pleased. England is better secured in this respect than any country, because every one who hold but 40s. a year for life has a vote for a Member of Parliament, by which, if he rent a farm, he is secure from oppression...

If all the forms in buying lands were abolished, every person almost who had got a little money would be ready to lay it out on land, and the land by passing through the different hands would be much better improved. There is no natural reason why a 1000 acres should not be as easily purchased as a 1000 yards of cloth. The keeping land out of the market always hinders its improvement. A merchant who buys a little piece of land has it in his eye to improve it and make the most of it he can. Great and ancient families have seldom either stock or inclination to improve their estates, except a small piece of pleasure ground about their house.

There are many errors in the police of almost every country, which have contributed greatly to stop the progress of agriculture. Our fathers, finding themselves once in every two or three years subject to the most grievous dearths, to escape that calamity prohibited the exportation of corn. This is still the police of the greater part of Europe, and it is the cause of all that dearth it is intended to prevent... All these causes have hindered and still hinder the improvement of agriculture, the most important branch of industry.

We may observe that the greater number of manufacturers there are in any country, agriculture is the more improved, and the causes which prevent the progress of these re-act, as it were, upon agriculture. It is easy to show that the free export and import of corn is favourable to agriculture. In England the country has been better stored with corn, and the price of it has gradually sunk, since the exportation of it was permitted. The bounty on exportation does harm in other respects, but it increases the quantity of corn. In Holland corn is cheaper and plentier than any where else, and a dearth is there unknown. That country is, as it were, the magazine of corn for a great part of Europe. This is entirely owing to the free export and import they enjoy. If no improper regulations took place, any country of Europe might do more than maintain itself with all sorts of grain.

The slow progress of arts and commerce is owing to causes of a like kind. In all places where slavery took place the manufactures were carried on by slaves. It is impossible that they can be so well carried on by slaves as by freemen, because they can have no motive to labour but the dread of punishment, and can never invent any machine for facilitating their business. Freemen who have a stock of their own can get any thing accomplished which they think may be expedient for carrying on labour. If a carpenter thinks that a plane will serve his purpose better than a knife, he may go to a smith and get it made; but if a slave make any such proposal he is called a lazy rascal, and no experiments are made to give him ease. At present the Turks and Hungarians work mines of the same kind, situated upon opposite sides of the same range of mountains, but the Hungarians make a great deal more of them than the Turks, because they employ freemen while the Turks employ slaves. When the Hungarians meet with any obstacle every invention is on work to find out some easy way of surmounting it, but the Turks think of no other expedient but to set a greater number of slaves to work. In the ancient world, as the arts were all carried on by slaves, no machinery could be invented, because they had no stock. After the fall of the Roman Empire, too, this was the case all over Europe.

In a rude society nothing is honourable but war. In the Odyssey, Ulysses is sometimes asked, by way of affront, whether he be a pirate or a merchant. At that time a merchant was reckoned odious and despicable. But a pirate or robber, as he was a man of military bravery, was treated with honour. We may observe that these principles of the human mind which are most beneficial to society are by no means marked by nature as the most honourable. Hunger, thirst, and the passion for sex are the great supports of the human species. Yet almost every expression of these excites contempt. In the same manner, that principle in the mind which prompts to truck, barter, and exchange, though it is the great foundation of arts, commerce, and the division of labour, yet it is not marked with any thing amiable. To perform any thing, or to give any thing, without a reward is always generous and noble, but to barter one thing for another is mean. The plain reason for this is that these principles are so strongly implanted by nature that they have no occasion for that additional force which the weaker principles need.

In rude ages this contempt rises to the highest pitch, and even in a refined society it is not utterly extinguished. In this country a small retailer is even in some degree odious at this day. When the trade of a merchant or mechanic was thus depreciated in the beginnings of society, no wonder that it was confined to the lowest ranks of people. Even when emancipated slaves began to practice these trades, it was impossible that much stock could accumulate in their hands, for the government oppressed them severely, and they were obliged to pay licenses for their liberty of trading. In Dooms–day–Book we have an account of all the different traders in every county, how many of them were under the king, and how many under such a bishop, and what acknowledgements they were obliged to pay for their liberty of trading.

This mean and despicable idea which they had of merchants greatly obstructed the progress of commerce. The merchant is, as it were, the mean between the manufacturer and the consumer. The weaver must not go to the market himself, there must be somebody to do this for him. This person must be possessed of a considerable stock, to buy up the commodity and maintain the manufacturer. But when merchants were so despicable and laid under so great taxations for liberty of trade, they could never amass that degree of stock which is necessary for making the division of labour and improving manufactures.

The only persons in these days who made any money by trade were the Jews, who, as they were considered as vagabonds, had no liberty of purchasing lands, and had no other way to dispose of themselves but by becoming mechanics or merchants. Their character could not be spoiled by merchandise because they could not be more odious than their religion made them. Even they were grievously oppressed and consequently the progress of opulence greatly retarded.

Another thing which greatly retarded commerce was the imperfection of the law with regard to contracts, which were the last species of rights that sustained action, for originally the law gave no redress for any but those concluded on the spot. At present all considerable commerce is carried on by commissions, and unless these sustained action little could be done. The first action on contracts extended only to the moveable goods of the contractor, neither his lands nor his person could be touched. His goods were often very inconsiderable, and probity is none of the most prevalent virtues among a rude people. It is commerce that introduces probity and punctuality.

Another obstacle to the improvement of commerce was the difficulty of conveyance from one place to another. The country was then filled with retainers, a species of idle people who depended on the lords, whose violence and disorders rendered the going from one place to another very difficult. Besides, there were then no good highways. The want of navigable rivers in many places were also an inconvenience. This is still the case in Asia and other eastern countries; all inland commerce is carried on by great caravans, consisting of several thousands, for mutual defense, with wagons, etc. In our own country a man made his testament before he set out from Edinburgh to Aberdeen, and it was still more dangerous to go to foreign countries. The laws of every country to aliens and strangers are far from being favourable. It is difficult, or rather impossible, for them to obtain satisfaction. After this was a little remedied, still conveyance by sea remained difficult. Piracy was an honourable occupation. Men were ignorant of navigation and exposed to dangers on this account. The price of all these risks was laid upon the goods, and by this means they were so much raised above the natural price that the improvement of commerce was greatly retarded.

Another piece of police which was thought a wise institution by our forefathers had the same effect. This was the fairs and markets all over Europe. Till the sixteenth century all commerce was carried on by fairs. The fairs of Bartholomew, of Leipsic, of Troy in Champaigne, and even of Glasgow, are much talked of in antiquity. These were the most central places and best fitted for carrying on business. All linen and black cattle were brought in from the country to these assignations or trysts, and, least the purchaser should be disappointed, they were all brought on a certain day and were not allowed to be sold on any other day. Forestallers, who went up and down the country buying up commodities, were severely punished, as this was a temptation not to bring them to the market. This might be necessary when it was not safe to go any where alone, but though you make no fairs, buyers and sellers will find a way to each other. Easy conveyance and other conveniences of trafficking will be of more advantage than the bringing them to a fixed market and thereby confining buying and selling to a certain season. All fairs, however necessary they then were, are now real nuisances. It is absurd to preserve in people a regard for their old customs when the causes of them are removed.

Another obstacle to commerce was staple towns, which had the exclusive privilege of selling a certain commodity within that district. Calais, when it belonged to the English, was long the staple for wool. As men were obliged to carry their wool to such a distance, its price was very high. It was however a very great advantage to any town to have the staple, and therefore the king gave it to that town with which he was best pleased, and took it away whenever it disobliged him. Staple-towns had all the disadvantages of fairs and markets with this additional one, that the staple commodity could be sold at no fair nor market except one. By this the liberty of exchange, and consequently the division of labour, was diminished.

All taxes upon exportation and importation of goods also hinder commerce. Merchants at first were in so contemptible a state that the law, as it were, abandoned them, and it was no matter what they obliged them to pay. They however must lay the tax upon their goods, their price is raised, fewer of them are bought, manufactures are discouraged, and the division of labour hindered.

All monopolies and exclusive privileges of corporations, for whatever good ends they were at first instituted, have the same bad effect. In like manner the statute of apprenticeship, which was originally an imposition on government, has a bad tendency. It was imagined that the cause of so much bad cloth was that the weaver had not been properly educated, and therefore they made a statute that he should serve a seven years apprenticeship before he pretended to make any. But this is by no means a sufficient security against bad cloth. You yourself cannot inspect a large piece of cloth, this must be left to the stampmaster, whose credit must be depended upon. Above all other causes the giving bounties for one commodity, and the discouraging another, diminishes the concurrence of opulence and hurts the natural state of commerce.

...

It remains now that we consider the last division of police, and show the influence of commerce on the manners of a people.

Whenever commerce is introduced into any country, probity and punctuality always accompany it. These virtues in a rude and barbarous country are almost unknown. Of all the nations in Europe, the Dutch, the most commercial, are the most faithful to their word. The English are more so than the Scotch, but much inferiour to the Dutch, and in the remote parts of this country they are far less so than in the commercial parts of it. This is not at all to be imputed to national character, as some pretend. There is no natural reason why an Englishman or a Scotchman should not be as punctual in performing agreements as a Dutchman. It is far more reducible to self interest, that general principle which regulates the actions of every man, and which leads men to act in a certain manner from views of advantage, and is as deeply implanted in an Englishman as a Dutchman. A dealer is afraid of losing his character, and is scrupulous in observing every engagement. When a person makes perhaps 20 contracts in a day, he cannot gain so much by endeavouring to impose on his neighbours, as the very appearance of a cheat would make him lose. Where people seldom deal with one another, we find that they are somewhat disposed to cheat, because they can gain more by a smart trick than they can lose by the injury which it does their character. They whom we call politicians are not the most remarkable men in the world for probity and punctuality. Ambassadors from different nations are still less so: they are praised for any little advantage they can take, and pique themselves a good deal on this degree of refinement. The reason of this is that nations treat with one another not above twice or thrice in a century, and they may gain more by one piece of fraud than lose by having a bad character. France has had this character with us ever since the reign of Lewis XIV, yet it has never in the least hurt either its interest or splendour.

But if states were obliged to treat once or twice a day, as merchants do, it would be necessary to be more precise in order to preserve their character. Wherever dealings are frequent, a man does not expect to gain so much by any one contract as by probity and punctuality in the whole, and a prudent dealer, who is sensible of his real interest, would rather choose to lose what he has a right to than give any ground for suspicion. Every thing of this kind is as odious as it is rare. When the greater part of people are merchants they always bring probity and punctuality into fashion, and these therefore are the principal virtues of a commercial nation.

There are some inconveniences, however, arising from a commercial spirit. The first we shall mention is that it confines the views of men. Where the division of labour is brought to perfection, every man has only a simple operation to perform. To this his whole attention is confined, and few ideas pass in his mind but what have an immediate connection with it. When the mind is employed about a variety of objects it is some how expanded and enlarged, and on this account a country artist is generally acknowledged to have a range of thoughts much above a city one. The former is perhaps a joiner, a house carpenter, and a cabinet maker all in one, and his attention must of course be employed about a number of objects of very different kinds. The latter is perhaps only a cabinet maker. That particular kind of work employs all his thoughts, and as he had not an opportunity of comparing a number of objects, his views of things beyond his own trade are by no means so extensive as those of the former. This must be much more the case when a person's whole attention is bestowed on the 17th part of a pin or the 80th part of a button, so far divided are these manufactures. It is remarkable that in every commercial nation the low people are exceedingly stupid. The Dutch vulgar are eminently so, and the English are more so than the Scotch. The rule is general, in towns they are not so intelligent as in the country, nor in a rich country as in a poor one.

Another inconvenience attending commerce is that education is greatly neglected. In rich and commercial nations the division of labour, having reduced all trades to very simple operations, affords an opportunity of employing children very young. In this country indeed, where the division of labour is not far advanced, even the meanest porter can read and write, because the price of education is cheap, and a parent can employ his child no other way at 6 or 7 years of age. This however is not the case in the commercial parts of England. A boy of 6 or 7 years of age at Brimingham can gain his 3 pence or sixpence a day, and parents find it to be their interest to set them soon to work. Thus their education is neglected. The education which low people's children receive is not indeed at any rate considerable; however, it does them an immense deal of service, and the want of it is certainly one of their greatest misfortunes. By it they learn to read, and this gives them the benefit of religion, which is a great advantage, not only considered in a pious sense, but as it affords them subject for thought and speculation. From this we may observe the benefit of country schools, and, however much neglected, must acknowledge them to be an excellent institution. But besides this want of education, there is another great loss which attends the putting boys too soon to work. The boy begins to find that his father is obliged to him, and therefore throws off his authority. When he is grown up he has no ideas with which he can amuse himself. When he is away from his work he must therefore betake himself to drunkenness and riot. Accordingly we find that in the commercial parts of England, the tradesmen are for the most part in this despicable condition: their work through half the week is sufficient to maintain them, and through want of education they have no amusement for the other but riot and debauchery. So it may very justly be said that the people who clothe the whole world are in rags themselves.

Another bad effect of commerce is that it sinks the courage of mankind, and tends to extinguish martial spirit. In all commercial countries the division of labour is infinite, and every one's thoughts are employed about one particular thing. In great trading towns, for example, the linen merchants are of several kinds, for the dealing in Hamburgh and Irish linens are quite distinct professions. Some of the lawyers attend at King's Bench, some at the Court of Common Pleas, and others at the Chauncery. Each of them is in a great measure unacquainted with the business of his neighbour. In the same manner war comes to be a trade also. A man has then time to study only one branch of business, and it would be a great disadvantage to oblige every one to learn the military art and keep himself in the practice of it. The defense of the country is therefore committed to a certain set of men who have nothing else ado; and among the bulk of the people military courage diminishes. By having their minds constantly employed on the arts of luxury, they grow effeminate and dastardly.

This is confirmed by universal experience. In the year 1745 four or 5 thousand naked unarmed Highlanders took possession of the improved parts of this country without any opposition from the unwarlike inhabitants. They penetrated into England and alarmed the whole nation, and had they not been opposed by a standing army they would have seized the throne with little difficulty. 200 years ago such an attempt would have roused the spirit of the nation. Our ancestors were brave and warlike, their minds were not enervated by cultivating arts and commerce, and they were already with spirit and vigor to resist the most formidable foe. It is for the same reason too that an army of 4 or 500 Europeans have often penetrated into the Mogul's country, and that the most numerous armies of the Chinese have always been overthrown by the Tartars. In these countries the division of labour and luxury have arrived at a very high pitch, they have no standing army, and the people are all intent on the arts of peace. Holland, were its barriers removed, would be an easy prey. In the beginning of this century the standing army of the Dutch was beat in the field, and the rest of the inhabitants, instead of rising in arms to defend themselves, formed a design of deserting their country and settling in the East Indies. A commercial country may be formidable abroad, and may defend itself by fleets and standing armies, but when they are overcome and the enemy penetrates into the country, the conquest is easy. The same observation may be made with respect to Rome and Carthage. The Carthaginians were often victorious abroad, but when the war was carried into their own country they had no share with the Romans. These are the disadvantages of a commercial spirit. The minds of men are contracted and rendered incapable of elevation, education is despised or at least neglected, and heroic spirit is almost utterly extinguished. To remedy these defects would be an object worthy of serious attention.

II. Governing the Market

… Three

James Steuart
(1712–1780)

AN INQUIRY INTO THE PRINCIPLES OF POLITICAL ECONOMY (1767)

Introduction

Economy, in general, is the art of providing for all the wants of a family, with prudence and frugality.

If any thing necessary or useful be found wanting, if any thing provided be lost or misapplied, if any servant, any animal, be supernumerary or useless, if any one sick or infirm be neglected, we immediately perceive a want of economy. The object of it, in a private family, is therefore to provide for the nourishment, the other wants, and the employment of every individual. In the first place, for the master, who is the head, and who directs the whole; next for the children, who interest him above all other things; and last for the servants, who being useful to the head, and essential to the well-being of the family, have therefore a title to become an object of the master's care and concern.

The whole economy must be directed by the head, who is both lord and steward of the family. It is however necessary, that these two offices be not confounded with one another. As lord, he establishes the laws of his economy; as steward, he puts them in execution. As lord, he may restrain and give his commands to all within the house as he thinks proper; as steward, he must conduct with gentleness and address, and is bound by his own regulations. The better the economist, the more uniformity is perceived in all his actions, and the less liberties are taken to depart from stated rules. He is not so much master, as that he may break through the laws of his economy, although in every respect he may keep each individual within the house, in the most exact subordination to his commands. Economy and government, even in a private family, present therefore two different ideas, and have also two different objects.

What economy is in a family, political economy is in a state: with these essential differences, however, that in a state there are no servants, all are children: that a family may be formed when and how a man pleases, and he may there establish what plan of economy he thinks fit; but states are found formed, and the economy of these depends upon a thousand circumstances. The statesman (this is a general term to signify the legislature and supreme power, according to the form of government) is neither master to establish what economy he pleases, or, in the exercise of his sublime authority, to overturn at will the established laws of it, let him be the most despotic monarch upon earth.

The great art therefore of political economy is, first to adapt the different operations of it to the spirit, manners, habits, and customs of the people; and afterwards to model these circumstances so, as to be able to introduce a set of new and more useful institutions.

The principal object of this science is to secure a certain fund of subsistence for all the inhabitants, to obviate every circumstance which may render it precarious; to provide every thing necessary for supplying the wants of the society, and to employ the inhabitants (supposing them to be free-men) in such a manner as naturally to create reciprocal relations and dependencies between them, so as to make their several interests lead them to supply one another with their reciprocal wants.

If one considers the variety which is found in different countries, in the distribution of property, subordination of classes, genius of people, proceeding from the variety of forms of government, laws, climate, and manners, one may conclude, that the political economy in each must necessarily be different, and that principles, however universally true, may become quite ineffectual in practice, without a sufficient preparation of the spirit of a people.

It is the business of a statesman to judge of the expediency of different schemes of economy, and by degrees to model the minds of his subjects so as to induce them, from the allurement of private interest, to concur in the execution of his plan.

The speculative person who, removed from the practice, extracts the principles of this science from *observation and reflection*, should divest himself, as far as possible, of every prejudice in favour of established opinions, however reasonable, when examined relatively to particular nations: he must do his utmost to become a citizen of the world, comparing customs, examining minutely institutions which appear alike, when in different countries they are found to produce different effects: he should examine the cause of such differences with the utmost diligence and attention. It is from such inquiries that the true principles are discovered.

He who takes up the pen upon this subject, keeping in his eye the customs of his own or any other country, will fall more naturally into a description of one particular system of it, than into an examination of the principles of the science in general; he will applaud such institutions as he finds rightly administered at home; he will condemn those which are administered with abuse; but, without comparing different methods of executing the same plan in different countries, he will not easily distinguish the disadvantages which are essential to the institution, from those which proceed from the abuse. For this reason a land-tax excites the indignation of a Frenchman, an excise that of an Englishman. One who looks into the execution of both, in each country, and in every branch of their management, will discover the real effects of these impositions, and be able to distinguish what proceeds from abuse, from what is essential to the burden.

Nothing is more effectual towards preparing the spirit of a people to receive a good plan of economy, than a proper representation of it.

Having pointed out the object of my pursuit, I shall only add, that my intention is to attach myself principally to a clear deduction of principles, and a short application of them to familiar examples, in order to avoid abstraction as much as possible. I farther intend to confine myself to such parts of this extensive subject, as shall appear the most interesting in the general system of modern politics; of which I shall treat with that spirit of liberty, which reigns more and more every day, throughout all the polite and flourishing nations of Europe…

I pretend to form no system, but, by tracing out a succession of principles, consistent with the nature of man and with one another, I shall endeavour to furnish some materials towards the forming of a good one.

Book I: Of Population and Agriculture

Chap. II: Of the Spirit of a People

The spirit of a people is formed upon a set of received opinions relative to three objects: morals, government, and manners; these once generally adopted by any society, confirmed by long and constant habit, and never called in question, form the basis of all laws, regulate the form of every government, and determine what is commonly called the customs of a country.

To know a people, we must examine them under these general heads. We acquire the knowledge of their morals with ease, by consulting the tenets of their religion, and from what is taught among them by authority.

The second, or government, is more disguised, as it is constantly changing from circumstances, partly resulting from domestic and partly from foreign considerations. A thorough knowledge of their history, and conversation with their ministers of state, may give one, who has access to these helps, a very competent knowledge of this branch.

The last, or the knowledge of the manners of a people, is by far the most difficult to acquire, and yet is the most open to every person's observation. Certain circumstances with regard to manners are supposed by every one in the country to be so well known, so generally followed and observed, that it seldom occurs to any body to inform a stranger concerning them. In one country nothing is so injurious as a stroke with a stick, or even a gesture which implies a design or a desire to strike. In another a stroke is not near so offensive as an opprobrious expression. An innocent liberty with the fair sex, which in one country passes without censure, is looked upon in another as the highest indignity. In general, the opinion of a people with regard to injuries is established by custom only, and nothing is more necessary in government, than an exact attention to every circumstance peculiar to the people to be governed... I need not enlarge upon this subject, my intention is only to suggest an idea which any one may pursue, and which will be applied upon many occasions as we go along; for there is no treating any point which regards the political economy of a nation, without accompanying the example with some supposition relative to the spirit of the people.

I have said, that the most difficult thing to learn concerning a people, is the spirit of their manners. Consequently, the most difficult thing for a stranger to adopt, is their manner. Men acquire the language, nay even lose the foreign accent, before they lose the peculiarity of their manner. The reason is plain. The inclinations must be changed, the taste for amusements must be new-modeled; established maxims upon government, manners, nay even upon some moral actions, must undergo certain new modifications, before the stranger's conversation and behaviour can become consistent with the spirit of the people with whom he lives.

From these considerations, we may find the reason, why nothing is more heavy to bear than the government of conquerors, in spite of all their endeavours to render themselves agreeable to the conquered. Of this, experience has ever proved the truth, and princes are so much persuaded of it, that when a country is subdued in our days, or when it otherwise changes masters, there is seldom any question of altering, but by very slow degrees and length of time, the established laws and customs of the inhabitants. I might safely say, there is no form of government upon earth so excellent in itself, as, necessarily, to make the people happy under it. Freedom itself, *imposed* upon a people groaning under the greatest slavery, will not make them happy, unless it is made to undergo certain modifications, relative to their established habits.

Having explained what I mean by the spirit of a people, I come next to consider, how far this spirit must influence government.

If governments be taken in general, we shall find them analogous to the spirit of the people. But the point under consideration is, how a statesman is to proceed, when expediency and refinement require a change of administration, or when it becomes necessary from a change of circumstances.

The great alteration in the affairs of Europe within these three centuries, by the discovery of America and the Indies, the springing up of industry and learning, the introduction of trade and the luxurious arts, the establishment of public credit, and a general system of taxation, have entirely altered the plan of government every where.

From feudal and military, it is become free and commercial. I oppose freedom in government to the feudal system, to mark only that there is not found now that chain of subordination among the subjects, which made the essential part of the feudal form. The head there had little power, and the lower classes of the people little liberty. Now every industrious man, who lives with economy, is free and independent under most forms of government. Formerly, the power of the barons swallowed up the independency of all inferior classes. I oppose commercial to military; because the military governments now are made to subsist from the consequences and effects of commerce only. That is, from the revenue of the state, proceeding from taxes. Formerly, every thing was brought about by numbers; now, numbers of men cannot be kept together without money.

This is sufficient to point out the nature of the revolution in the political state, and of consequence in the manners of Europe.

The spirit of a people changes no doubt of itself, but by slow degrees. The same generation commonly adheres to the same principles, and retains the same spirit. In every country we find two generations upon the stage at a time; that is to say, we may distribute into two classes the spirit which prevails; the one amongst men between twenty and thirty, when opinions are forming; the other of those who are past fifty, when opinions and habits are formed and confirmed. A person of judgment and observation may foresee many things relative to government, from an exact attention to the rise and progress of new customs and opinions, provided he preserve his mind free from all attachments and prejudices, in favour of those which he himself has adopted, and in that delicacy of sensation necessary to perceive the influence of a change of circumstances. This is the genius proper to form a great minister.

In every new step the spirit of the people should be first examined; and if this be not found ripe for the execution of the plan, it ought to be put off, kept entirely secret, and every method used to prepare the people to relish the innovation...

In turning and working upon the spirit of a people, nothing is impossible to an able statesman. When a people can be engaged to murder their wives and children, and to burn themselves, rather than submit to a foreign enemy, when they can be brought to give their most precious effects, their ornaments of gold and silver, for the support of a common cause; when women are brought to give their hair to make ropes, and the most decrepit old men to mount the walls of a town for its defense; I think I may say, that by properly conducting and managing the spirit of a people nothing is impossible to be accomplished. But when I say, nothing is impossible, I must be understood to mean, that nothing essentially necessary for the good of the people is impossible; and this is all that is required in government...

The great art of governing is to divest oneself of prejudices and attachments to particular opinions, particular classes, and above all to particular persons; to consult the spirit of the people, to give way to it in appearance, and in so doing to give it a turn capable of inspiring those sentiments which may induce them to relish the change, which an alteration of circumstances has rendered necessary.

Can any change be greater among free men, than from a state of absolute liberty and independence to become subject to constraint in the most trivial actions? This change has however taken place over all Europe within these three hundred years, and yet we think ourselves more free than ever our fathers were. Formerly a gentleman who enjoyed a bit of land, knew not what it was to have any demand made upon him, but in virtue of obligations by himself contracted. He disposed of the fruits of the earth, and of the labour of his servants or vassals, as he thought fit. Every thing was bought, sold, transferred, transported, modified, and composed, for private consumption, or for public use, without ever the state's being once found interested in what was doing. This, I say, was formerly the general situation of Europe, among free nations under a regular administration; and the only impositions commonly known to affect landed men, were made in consequence of a contract of subordination, feudal or other, which had certain limitations; and the impositions were appropriated for certain purposes.

Daily experience shows, that nothing is more against the inclinations of a people than the imposition of taxes; and the less they are accustomed to them, the more difficult it is to get them established.

The great abuse of governors in the application of taxes contributes not a little to entertain and augment this repugnancy in the governed: but besides abuse, there is often too little management used to prepare the spirits of the people for such innovations; for we see them upon many occasions submitting with cheerfulness to very heavy impositions, provided they be well-timed, and consistent with their manners and disposition...

It often happens, that statesmen take the hint of new impositions from the example of other nations, and not from a nice examination of their own domestic circumstances. But when these are rightly attended to, it becomes easy to discover the means of executing the same plan, in a way quite adapted to the spirit, temper, and circumstances of the people. When strangers are employed as statesmen, the disorder is still greater, unless there be extraordinary penetration, temper, and, above all, flexibility and discretion.

Statesmen have sometimes recourse to artifice instead of reason, because their intentions often are not upright. This destroys all confidence between them and the people; and confidence is necessary when you are in a manner obliged to ask a favour, or when what you demand is not indisputably your right. A people thus tricked into an imposition, though expedient for their prosperity, will oppose violently, at another time, a like measure, even when essential to their preservation.

At other times, we see statesmen presenting the allurement of present ease, precisely at the time when people's minds are best disposed to receive a burden. I mean when war threatens, and when the mind is heated with a resentment of injuries. Is it not wonderful, at such a time as this, to increase taxes in proportion only to the interest of money wanted; does not this imply a short-sightedness, or at least an indifference as to what is to come? Is it not more natural, that a people should consent to come under burdens to gratify revenge, than submit to repay a large debt when their minds are restored to a state of tranquility?

From the examples I have given, I hope what I mean by the spirit of a people is sufficiently understood, and I think I have abundantly shown the necessity of its being properly disposed, in order to establish a right plan of economy. This is so true, that many examples may be found, of a people's rejecting the most beneficial institutions, and even the greatest favours, merely because some circumstance had shocked their established customs. No wonder then, if we see them refuse to come under limitations, restraints, and burdens, when the utmost they can be flattered with from them, is a distant prospect of national good...

[Plan of Political Economy]

In order to communicate an adequate idea of what I understand by political economy, I have explained the term, by pointing out the object of the art; which is, to provide food, other necessaries, and employment to every one of the society.

This is a very simple and a very general method of defining a most complicated operation. To provide a proper employment for all the members of a society, is the same as to model and conduct every branch of their concerns.

Upon this idea may be formed, I think, the most extensive basis for an inquiry into the principles of political economy.

The next thing to be done, is to fall upon a distinct method of analysing so extensive a subject, by contriving a train of ideas, which may be directed towards every part of the plan, and which, at the same time, may be made to arise methodically from one another.

For this purpose I have taken a hint from what the late revolutions in the politics of Europe have pointed out to be the regular progress of mankind, from great simplicity to complicated refinement.

This first book shall then set out with taking up society in the cradle, as I may say. I shall here examine the principles which influence their multiplication, the method of providing for their subsistence, the origin of their labour, the effects of their liberty and slavery, the distribution of them into classes, with some other topics which relate to mankind in general.

Here we shall find the principles of industry influencing the multiplication of mankind, and the cultivation of the soil. This I have thrown in on purpose to prepare my reader for the subject of the second book; where he will find the same principle (under the wings of liberty) providing an easy subsistence for a numerous populace, by the means of trade, which sends the labour of an industrious people over the whole world.

From the experience of what has happened these last two hundred years, we find to what a pitch the trade and industry of Europe has increased alienations, and the circulation of money. I shall therefore closely adhere to these, as the most immediate consequences of the preceding improvement; and, by analysing them, I shall form my third and fourth books, in which I intend to treat of money and credit.

We see also how credit has engaged nations to avail themselves of it in their wars, and how, by the use of it, they have been led to contract debts; which they never can satisfy and pay, without imposing taxes. The doctrine, then, of debts and taxes will very naturally follow that of credit in this great chain of political consequences...

Book II: Of Trade and Industry

Introduction

...

[Self-interest]

Now the relations between the different principles of which I treat, are indeed striking to such as are accustomed to abstract reasoning, but not near so much as when the application of them is made to different examples.

The principle of self-interest will serve as a general key to this inquiry; and it may, in one sense, be considered as the ruling principle of my subject, and may therefore be traced throughout the whole. This is the main spring, and only motive which a statesman should make use of, to engage a free people to concur in the plans which he lays down for their government.

I beg I may not here be understood to mean, that self-interest should conduct the statesman: by no means. Self-interest, when considered with regard to him, is public spirit; and it can only be called self-interest, when it is applied to those who are to be governed by it.

...

I have said that self-interest is the ruling principle of my subject, and I have so explained myself, as to prevent any one from supposing, that I consider it as the universal spring of human actions. Here is the light in which I want to represent this matter.

The best way to govern a society, and to engage every one to conduct himself according to a plan, is for the statesman to form a system of administration, the most consistent possible with the interest of every individual, and never to flatter himself that his people will be brought to act in general, and in matters which purely regard the public, from any other principle than private interest. This is the utmost length to which I pretend to carry my position. As to what regards the merit and demerit of actions in general, I think it fully as absurd to say, that no action is truly virtuous, as to affirm, that none is really vicious.

It might perhaps be expected, that, in treating of politics, I should have brought in public spirit also, as a principle of action; whereas all I require with respect to this principle is merely a restraint from it; and even this is, perhaps, too much to be taken for granted. Were public spirit, instead of private utility, to become the spring of action in the individuals of a well-governed state, I apprehend, it would spoil all. Let me explain myself.

Public spirit, in my way of treating this subject, is as superfluous in the governed, as it ought to be all-powerful in the statesman; at least, if it is not altogether superfluous, it is fully as much so, as miracles are in a religion once fully established. Both are admirable at setting out, but would shake every thing loose, were they to continue to be common and familiar. Were miracles wrought every day, the laws of nature would no longer be laws: and were every one to act for the public, and neglect himself, the statesman would be bewildered, and the supposition is ridiculous.

I expect, therefore, that every man is to act for his own interest in what regards the public; and, politically speaking, every one ought to do so. It is the combination of every private interest which forms the public good, and of this the public, that is, the statesman only, can judge. You must love your country. Why? Because it is yours. But you must not prefer your own interest to that of your country. This, I agree, is perfectly just and right: but this means no more, than that you are to abstain from acting to its prejudice, even though your own private interest should demand it; that is, you should abstain from unlawful gain. Count Julian, for example, who, from private resentment, it is said, brought the Moors into Spain, and ruined his country, transgressed this maxim. A spy in an army, or in a cabinet, who betrays the secrets of his country, and he who sells his trust, are in the same case: defrauding the state is, among many others, a notorious example of this. To suppose men, in general, honest in such matters, would be absurd. The legislature therefore ought to make good laws, and those who transgress them ought to be speedily, severely, and most certainly punished. This belongs to the coercive part of government, and, falling beyond the limits of my subject, is ever taken for granted.

Were the principle of public spirit carried farther; were a people to become quite disinterested; there would be no possibility of governing them. Every one might consider the interest of his country in a different light, and many might join in the ruin of it, by endeavouring to promote its advantages. Were a rich merchant to begin and sell his goods without profit, what would become of trade? Were another to defray the extraordinary expense of some workmen in a hard year, in order to enable them to carry on their industry, without raising their price, what would become of others, who had not the like advantages? Were a man of a large landed estate to sell his grain at a low price in a year of scarcity, what would become of the poor farmers? Were people to feed all who would ask charity, what would become of industry? These operations of public spirit ought to be left to the public, and all that is required of individuals is, not to endeavour to defeat them.

This is the regular distribution of things, and it is this only which comes under my consideration...

The less attentive any government is to do *their* duty, the more essential it is that every individual be animated by *that* spirit, which then languishes in the very part where it ought to flourish with the greatest strength and vigour; and on the other hand, the more public spirit is shown in the administration of public affairs, the less occasion has the state for assistance from individuals...

Chap. X: Of the Balance of Work and Demand

It is quite impossible to go methodically through the subject of political economy, without being led into anticipations. We have frequently mentioned this balance of work and demand, and showed how important a matter it is for a statesman to attend to it. The thing, therefore, in general is well understood; and all that remains to be done, is to render our ideas more determinate concerning it, and more adequate, if possible, to the principles we have been laying down...

The word demand in this chapter is taken in the most simple acceptation; and when we say that the balance between work and demand is to be sustained in equilibrio, as far as possible, we mean that the quantity supplied should be in proportion to the quantity *demanded*, that is, *wanted*. While the balance stands justly poised, prices are found in the adequate proportion of the real expense of making the goods, with a small addition for profit to the manufacturer and merchant.

I have, in the fourth chapter, observed how necessary a thing it is to distinguish the two constituent parts of every price; the value, and the profit. Let the number of persons be ever so great, who, upon the sale of a piece of goods, share in the profits; it is still essential, in such enquiries as these, to suppose them distinctly separate from the real value of the commodity; and the best way possible to discover exactly the proportion between the one and the other, is by a scrupulous watchfulness over the balance we are now treating of, as we shall presently see.

The value and profits, combined in the price of a manufacture produced by one man, are easily distinguished by means of the analysis we have laid down in the fourth chapter. As long as any market is *fully* supplied with this sort of work, and *no more*; those who are employed in it live by their trade, and gain no unreasonable profit: because there is then no violent competition upon one side only, neither between the workmen, nor between those who buy from them, and the balance gently vibrates under the influence of a double competition. This is the representation of a perfect balance.

This balance is overturned in four different ways:

Either the demand diminishes, and the work remains the same;

Or the work diminishes, and the demand remains;

Or the demand increases, and the work remains;

Or the work increases, and the demand remains.

Now each of these four relations between demand and work may, or may not, produce a competition upon one side of the contract only. This must be explained.

If demand diminishes, and work remains the same, which is the first case, either those who furnish the work will enter into competition, in which case they will hurt each other, and prices will fall below the reasonable standard of the even balance; or they will not enter into competition, and then prices continuing as formerly, the whole demand will be supplied, and the remainder of the work will lie upon hand.

This is a symptom of decaying trade.

Let us now, on the other hand, suppose demand to increase, and work to remain as before.

This example points out no diminution on either side, as was the case before, but an augmentation upon one; and is either a symptom of growing luxury at home, or of an increase in foreign trade.

Here the same alternation of circumstances occurs. The demanders will either enter into competition and raise the price of work, or they will enter into no competition; but being determined not to exceed the ordinary standard of the perfect balance, will defer making their provision till another time, or supply themselves in another market; that is to say, the new demand will cease as soon as it is made, for want of a supply.

Whenever, therefore, this perfect balance of work and demand is overturned by the force of a simple competition, or by one of the scale preponderating, one of two things must happen; either a part of the demand is not answered, or a part of the goods is not sold.

These are the immediate effects of the overturning of the balance.

Let me next point out the object of the statesman's care, relatively to such effects, and show the consequences of their being neglected.

We may now simplify our ideas, and instead of the former, make use of other expressions which may convey them.

Let us therefore say, that the *fall* or *rise* upon either side of the balance, is *positive*, or *relative*. *Positive*, when the side we talk of really augments beyond, or diminishes below the usual standard. *Relative*, when there is no alteration upon the side we speak of, and that the subversion of the balance is owing to an alteration on the other side. As for example:

Instead of saying demand diminishes, and work remains the same, let us say, demand diminishes *positively*, or work increases *relatively*; according as the subject may lead us to speak either of the one or of the other. This being premised.

If the scale of work shall preponderate *positively*, it should be inquired, whether the quantity furnished has really swelled, in all respects, beyond the proportion of the consumption, (in which case the statesman should diminish the number of hands, by throwing a part of them into a new channel) or whether the imprudence only of the workmen has made them produce their work unseasonably; in which case proper information and even assistance should be given them, to prevent merchants from taking advantage of their want of experience: but these last precautions are necessary in the infancy of industry only.

If a statesman should be negligent on this occasion; if he should allow natural consequences to follow upon one another, just as circumstances shall determine; then it may happen, that workmen will keep upon hand that part of their goods which exceeds the demand, until necessity forces them to enter into competition with one another, and sell for what they can get. Now this competition is hurtful, because it is all on one side, and because we have supposed the prepondering of the scale of work to be an overturning of a perfect balance, which can by no means be set right, consistently with a scheme of thriving, but by the scale of demand becoming heavier, and re-establishing a double competition. Were this to happen before the workmen come to sell in competition, then the balance would again be even, after what I call a *short vibration*, which is no *subversion*; but when the scale of work remains too long in the same position, and occasions a strong, hurtful, and lasting competition, upon one side only, then, I say, the balance is *overturned*; because this diminishes the reasonable profits, or perhaps, indeed, obliges the workmen to sell below prime cost. The effect of this is, that the workmen fall into distress, and that industry suffers a discouragement; and this effect is certain.

But it may be asked, whether, by this fall of prices, demand will not be increased? That is to say, will not the whole of the goods be sold off?

I answer, that this may, or may not, be the effect of the fall, according to circumstances: it is a contingent consequence of the simple, but not the certain effect of the double competition: but the distress of the workmen is a certain and unavoidable consequence of the simple competition. But supposing this contingent consequence to happen, will it not set the balance even, by increasing the demand? I answer, the balance is then made even by a violent shock given to industry, but it is not set even from any principle which can support it, or make it flourish. Here is the criterion of a perfect balance: *A positive moderate profit must balance a positive moderate profit; the balance must vibrate, and no loss must be found on either side.* In the example before us, the balance stands even, it is true; the work and the demand are equally poised as to quantity; but it is a *relative profit*, which hangs in the scale, opposite to a *relative loss*. I wish this may be well understood; farther illustrations will make it clear.

Next, let me suppose the scale of *demand* to preponderate positively. In this case, the statesman should be still more upon his guard, to provide a proportional supply; because the danger here may at first put on a show of profit, and deceive him.

The consequences of this subversion of the balance are either,

First, that a competition will take place among the demanders only, which will raise profits. Now if, after a short vibration, the supply comes to be increased by the statesman's care, no harm will ensue; competition will change sides, and profits will come down again to the perfect standard. But if the scale of demand remains preponderating, and so keeps profits high, the consequence will be, that, in a little time, not only the immediate seller of the goods, but also every one who has contributed to the manufacture, will insist upon sharing these new profits. Now the evil is not, that every one should share, or that the profits should swell, as long as they are supported by demand, and as long as they can truly be considered as precarious; but the mischief is, that, in consequence of this wide repartition, and by such profits subsisting for a long time, they insensibly become *consolidated*, or, as it were, transformed into the intrinsic value of the goods. This, I say, is brought about by time; because the habitual extraordinary gains of every one employed induce the more luxurious among them to change their way of life insensibly, and fall into the habit of making greater consumptions, and engage the more slothful to remain idle, till they are exhausted. When therefore it happens, that large profits have been made for a considerable time, and that they have had the effect of forming a taste for a more expensive way of living among the industrious, it will not be the cessation of the demand, nor the swelling of the supply, which will engage them to part with their gains. Nothing will produce this effect but sharp necessity; and the bringing down of their profits, and the throwing the workmen into distress, are then simultaneous; which proves the truth of what I have said, that these profits become, by long habit, virtually *consolidated* with the real value of the merchandise. These are the consequences of a neglected simple competition, which raises the profits upon industry, and keeps the balance overturned for a considerable time.

Secondly, let me examine the consequences of this overturn in the actual preponderancy of demand, when it does not occasion a competition among the demanders, and consequently, when it does not increase the profits upon industry.

This case can only happen, when the commodity is not a matter of great necessity, or even of great use; since the desire of procuring it is not sufficient to engage the buyers to raise their price; unless, indeed, this difference should proceed from the ease of providing the same, in other markets, as cheap as formerly. This last is a dangerous circumstance, and loudly calls for the attention of the statesman. He must prevent the desertion of the market, by a speedy supply for all the demand, and must even perhaps give encouragement to manufacturers, to enable them to diminish the prices fixed by the regular standard. This is the situation of a nation which is in the way of losing branches of her foreign trade; of which afterwards.

Whatever therefore be the consequences of the actual preponderancy of the scale of demand; that is, whether it tend to raise profits, or to discredit the market; the statesman's care should be directed immediately towards making the balance come even of itself, without any shock, and that as soon as possible, by increasing the supply. For if it be allowed to stand long in this overturned state, natural consequences will operate a forced restitution; that is, the rise in the price, or the call of a foreign market, will effectually cut off a proportional part of the demand, and leave the balance in an equilibrium, disadvantageous to trade and industry.

In the former case, the manufacturers were forced to starve, by a natural restitution, when the relative profits and loss of individuals balanced one another. Here the manufacturers are enriched for a little time, by a rise of profits, relative to the loss the nation sustains, by not supplying the whole demand. This results from the competition of their customers; but as soon as these profits become *consolidated* with the intrinsic value, they will cease to have the advantage of profits, and, becoming in a manner necessary to the existence of the goods, will cease to be considered as advantageous. These forced restitutions then, brought about, as we have said, by selling goods below their value, by cutting off a part of the demand, or by sending it to another market, resembles the operation of a carrier, who sets his ass's burden even, by laying a stone upon the lightest end of it. He however loses none of his merchandise; but the absurdity of the statesman is still greater, for he appears willingly to open the heavy end of the load, and to throw part of his merchandise into the highway.

I hope, by this time, I have sufficiently shown the difference in effect between the *simple* and the *double* competition; between the vibrations of this balance of work and demand, and the *overturning* of it. When it vibrates in moderation, and by short alternate risings and sinkings, then industry and trade go on prosperously, and are in harmony with each other; because both parties gain. The industrious man is recompensed in proportion to his ingenuity; the intrinsic value of goods does not vary, nor deceive the merchant; profits on both sides fluctuate according to demand, but never get time to consolidate with, and swell the real value, and never altogether disappear, and starve the workman.

This happy state cannot be supported but by the care of the statesman; and when he is found negligent in the discharge of this part of his duty, the consequence is, that either the spirit of industry, which, it is supposed, has cost him much pains to cultivate, is extinguished, or the produce of it rises to so high a value, as to be out of the reach of a multitude of purchasers.

The progress towards the one or the other of these extremes is easily perceived, by attending to the successive overturnings of the balance. When these are often repeated on the same side, and the balance set right, by a succession of forced restitutions only, the same scale preponderating a-new, then is the last period soon accomplished. When, on the contrary, the overturnings are alternate, sometimes the scale of demand overturning the balance, sometimes the scale of work, the last period is more distant. Trade and industry subsist longer, but they remain in a state of perpetual convulsion. On the other hand, when the balance gently vibrates, then work and demand, that is, trade and industry, like agriculture and population, prove mutually assisting to each other, in promoting their reciprocal augmentation.

In order therefore to preserve a trading state from decline, the greatest care must be taken, to support a perfect balance between the hands employed in work and the demand for their labour. That is to say, according to former definitions, to prevent demand from ever standing long at an immoderate height, by providing at all times a supply, sufficient to answer the greatest that ever can be made: or, in other words, still, in order to accustom my readers to certain expressions, to encourage the *great*, and to discourage the *high* demand. In this case, competition will never be found too strong on either side of the contract, and profits will be moderate, but sure, on both.

If, on the contrary, there be found too many hands for the demand, work will fall too low for workmen to be able to live; or, if there be too few, work will rise, and manufactures will not be exported.

For want of this just balance, no trading state has ever been of long duration, after arriving at a certain height of prosperity. We perceive in history the rise, progress, grandeur, and decline of Sydon, Tyre, Carthage, Alexandria, and Venice, not to come nearer home. While these states were on the growing hand, they were powerful; when once they came to their height, they immediately found themselves labouring under their own greatness. The reason of this appears from what has been said.

While there is a demand for the trade of any country, inhabitants are always on the increasing hand. This is evident from what has been so often repeated in the first book, and confirmed by thousands of examples. There never was any branch of trade established in any kingdom, province, city, or even village; but such kingdoms, province, etc. increased in inhabitants. While this gradual increase of people is in proportion to the growing demand for hands, the balance between work and demand is exactly kept up; but as all augmentations must at last come to a stop, when this happens, inconveniences must ensue, greater or less, according to the negligence or attention of the statesman, and the violence or suddenness of the revolution.

Chap. XI: Why in Time this Balance is Destroyed

Let us now examine what may be the reason why, in a trading and industrious nation, time necessarily destroys the perfect balance between work and demand.

We have already pointed out one general cause, to wit, the natural stop which must at last be put to augmentations of every kind.

Let us now apply this to circumstances, in order to discover in what manner natural causes operate this stop, either by preventing the increase of work, on one side of the balance, or the increase of demand, on the other. When once we discover how the stop is put to augmentations, we may safely conclude, that the continuation of the same, or similar causes, will soon produce a diminution, and operate a decline.

We have traced the progress of industry, and shown how it goes hand in hand with the augmentation of subsistence, which is the principal allurement to labour. Now the augmentation of food is relative to the soil, and as long as this can be brought to produce, at an expense proportioned to the value of the returns, agriculture, without any doubt, will go forward in every country of industry. But so soon as the progress of agriculture demands an additional expense, which the natural return, at the stated prices of subsistence, will not defray, agriculture comes to a stop, and so would numbers, did not the consequences of industry push them forward, in spite of small difficulties. The industrious then, I say, continue to multiply, and the consequence is, that food becomes scarce, and that the inhabitants enter into competition for it.

This is no contingent consequence, it is an infallible one; because food is an article of the first necessity, and here the provision is supposed to fall short of demand. This raises the profits of those who have food ready to sell; and as the balance upon this article must remain overturned for some time, without the interposition of the statesman, these profits will be consolidated with the price, and give encouragement to a more expensive improvement of the soil. I shall here interrupt the examination of the consequences of this revolution as to agriculture, until I have examined the effects which the rise of the price of food produces on industry, and on the demand for it.

This augmentation on the value of subsistence must necessarily raise the price of all work, because we are here speaking of an industrious people fully employed, and because subsistence is one of the three articles which compose the intrinsic value of their work, as has been said.

The rise therefore, upon the price of work, not being any augmentation of that part of the price which we call profits, as happens to be the case when a rise in demand has produced a competition among the buyers, cannot be brought down but by increasing the supply of subsistence; and were a statesman to mistake the real cause of the rise, and apply the remedy of increasing the quantity of work, in order to bring down the market, instead of augmenting the subsistence, he would occasion a great disorder; he would introduce the hurtful simple competition between people who labour for moderate profits, mentioned in the last chapter, and would throw such a discouragement upon their industry, as would quickly extinguish it altogether.

On the other hand, did he imprudently augment the subsistence, by large importations, he would put an end to the expensive improvements of the soil, and this whole enterprise would fall to nothing. Here then is a dilemma, out of which he can extricate himself by a right application of public money, only.

Such a necessary rise in the price of labour may either affect foreign exportation, or it may not, according to circumstances. If it does, the price of subsistence, at any rate, must be brought down at least to those who supply the foreign demand; if it does not affect foreign exportation, matters may be allowed to go on; but still the remedy must be ready at hand, to be applied the moment it becomes expedient.

There is one necessary augmentation upon the prices of industry, brought about by a very natural cause, viz. the increase of population, which may imply a more expensive improvement of the soil; that is, an extension of agriculture. This augmentation may very probably put a stop to the augmentation of demand for many branches of manufactures, consequently may stop the progress of industry; and if the same causes continue to operate in a greater degree, it may also cut off a part of the former demand, may discredit the market, open a door to foreign consumption, and produce the inconveniences of poverty and distress, in proportion to the degree of negligence in the statesman.

I shall now give another example, of a very natural augmentation upon the intrinsic value of work, which does not proceed from the increase of population, but from the progress of industry itself; which implies no internal vice in a state, but which is the necessary consequence of the reformation of a very great one. This augmentation must be felt less or more in every country, in proportion as industry becomes extended.

We have said, that the introduction of manufactures naturally tends to purge the lands of superfluous mouths: now this is a very slow and gradual operation. A consequence of it was said to be (Book I, Chap. xx) an augmentation of the price of labour, because those who have been purged off, must begin to gain their whole subsistence at the expense of those who employ them.

If therefore, in the infancy of industry, any branch of it shall find itself assisted in a particular province, by the cheap labour of those mouths superfluously fed by the land, examples of which are very frequent, this advantage must diminish, in proportion as the cause of it ceases; that is, in proportion as industry is extended, and as the superfluous mouths are of consequence purged off.

This circumstance is of the last importance to be attended to by a statesman. Perhaps it was entirely owing to it, that industry was enabled to set up its head in this corner. How many examples could I give, of this assistance given to manufactures in different provinces, where I have found the value of a day's work, of spinning, for example, not equal to half the nourishment of the person. This is a great encouragement to the making of cloths; and accordingly we see some infant manufactures dispute the market with the produce of the greatest dexterity; the distaff dispute prices with the wheel. But when these provinces come to be purged of their superfluous mouths, spinning becomes a trade, and the spinners must live by it. Must not then prices naturally rise? And if these are not supported by the statesman, or if assistance is not given to these poor manufacturers, to enable them to increase their dexterity, in order to compensate what they are losing in cheapness, will not their industry fail? Will not the poor spinners be extinguished? For it is not to be expected, that the landlord will receive them back again from a principle of charity, after he has discovered their former uselessness.

A third cause of a necessary augmentation upon the intrinsic value of goods proceeds from taxes. A statesman must be very negligent indeed, if he does not attend to the immediate consequences of his own proper operations. I shall not enlarge on this at present, as it would be a necessary anticipation; but I shall return, to resume the part of my reasoning which I broke off abruptly.

I have observed, how the same cause which stops the progress of industry, gives an encouragement to agriculture: how the rise in the price of subsistence necessarily increases the price of work to an industrious and well-employed people: how this cuts off a part of the demand for work, or sends it to a foreign market.

Now all these consequences are entirely just, and yet they seem contradictory to another part of my reasoning, (Book I, Chap. xvi) where I set forth the advantages of a prodigal consumption of the earth's produce as advantageous to agriculture, by increasing the price of subsistence, without taking notice, on the other hand, of the hurt thereby done to industry, which supports the consumption of that produce.

The one and the other chain of consequences are equally just, and they appear contradictory upon the supposition only, that there is no statesman at the helm. These contradictions represent the alternate overturn of the balance. The duty of the statesman is, to support the double competition every where, and to permit the gentle alternate vibrations only of the two scales.

When the progress of industry has augmented numbers, and made subsistence scarce, he must estimate to what height it is expedient that the price of subsistence should rise. If he finds, that, in order to encourage the breaking up of new lands, the price of it must rise too high and stand high too long, to preserve the intrinsic value of goods at the same standard as formerly; then he must assist agriculture with his purse, in order that exportation may not be discouraged. This will have the effect of increasing subsistence, according to the true proportion of the augmentation required, without raising the price of it too high. And if this operation be the work of time, and the demand for the augmentation be pressing, he must continue to assist his agriculture and have subsistence imported, or brought from abroad, during that interval. This supply he may cut off whenever he pleases, that is, whenever it ceases to be necessary.

If the supply comes from a sister country, it must be so taken, as to occasion no violent revolution when it comes to be interrupted a-new. As for example: One province demands a supply of grain from another, for a few years only, until their own soil can be improved, so as to provide them sufficiently. The statesman should encourage agriculture, no doubt, in the province furnishing, and let the farmers know the extent of the demand, and the time it may probably last, as near as possible; but he must discourage the plucking up of vineyards, and even perhaps the breaking up of great quantities of old pasture; because, upon the ceasing of the demand, such changes upon the agriculture of the province furnishing, may occasion a hurtful revolution.

While this foreign supply is allowed to come in, the statesman should be closely employed in giving such encouragement to agriculture at home, according to the principles hereafter to be deduced, as may nearly balance the discouragement given to it by this newly permitted importation. If this step be neglected, the consequence may be, that the foreign supply will go on increasing every year, and will extinguish the agriculture already established in the country, instead of supplying a temporary exigency, which is within the power of the country itself to furnish. These, I suppose, were the principles attended to by the government of England, upon opening their ports for the importation of provisions from Ireland.

The principle, therefore, being to support a gentle increase of food, inhabitants, work, and demand, the statesman must suffer small vibrations in the balance, which, by alternate competition, may favour both sides of the contract; but whenever the competition stands too long upon either side, and threatens a subversion of the balance, then, with an artful hand, he must endeavour to load the lighter scale, and never, but in cases of the greatest necessity, have recourse to the expedient of taking any thing from the heavier.

# Four
Adam Ferguson
(1723–1816)

AN ESSAY ON THE HISTORY OF CIVIL SOCIETY
(1767)

PART IV: Of Consequences That Result from the Advancement of Civil and Commercial Arts

SECTION I: Of the Separation of Arts and Professions

It is evident, that, however urged by a sense of necessity, and a desire of convenience, or favoured by any advantages of situation and policy, a people can make no great progress in cultivating the arts of life, until they have separated, and committed to different persons, the several tasks, which require a peculiar skill and attention. The savage, or the barbarian, who must build and plant, and fabricate for himself, prefers, in the interval of great alarms and fatigues, the enjoyments of sloth to the improvement of his fortune: he is, perhaps, by the diversity of his wants, discouraged from industry; or, by his divided attention, prevented from acquiring skill in the management of any particular subject.

The enjoyment of peace, however, and the prospect of being able to exchange one commodity for another, turns, by degrees, the hunter and the warrior into a tradesman and a merchant. The accidents which distribute the means of subsistence unequally, inclination, and favourable opportunities, assign the different occupations of men; and a sense of utility leads them, without end, to subdivide their professions.

The artist finds, that the more he can confine his attention to a particular part of any work, his productions are the more perfect, and grow under his hands in the greater quantities. Every undertaker in manufacture finds, that the more he can subdivide the tasks of his workmen, and the more hands he can employ on separate articles, the more are his expenses diminished, and his profits increased. The consumer too requires, in every kind of commodity, a workmanship more perfect than hands employed on a variety of subjects can produce; and the progress of commerce is but a continued subdivision of the mechanical arts.

Every craft may engross the whole of a man's attention, and has a mystery which must be studied or learned by a regular apprenticeship. Nations of tradesmen come to consist of members who, beyond their own particular trade, are ignorant of all human affairs, and who may contribute to the preservation and enlargement of their commonwealth, without making its interest an object of their regard or attention. Every individual is distinguished by his calling, and has a place to which he is fitted. The savage, who knows no distinction but that of his merit, of his sex, or of his species, and to whom his community is the sovereign object of affection, is astonished to find, that in a scene of this nature, his being a man does not qualify him for any station whatever: he flies to the woods with amazement, distaste, and aversion.

By the separation of arts and professions, the sources of wealth are laid open; every species of material is wrought up to the greatest perfection, and every commodity is produced in the greatest abundance. The state may estimate its profits and its revenues by the number of its people. It may procure, by its treasure, that national consideration and power, which the savage maintains at the expense of his blood.

The advantage gained in the inferior branches of manufacture by the separation of their parts, seem to be equaled by those which arise from a similar device in the higher departments of policy and war. The soldier is relieved from every care but that of his service; statesmen divide the business of civil government into shares; and the servants of the public, in every office, without being skilful in the affairs of state, may succeed, by observing forms which are already established on the experience of others. They are made, like the parts of an engine, to concur to a purpose, without any concert of their own: and, equally blind with the trader to any general combination, they unite with him, in furnishing to the state its resources, its conduct, and its force.

The artifices of the beaver, the ant, and the bee, are ascribed to the wisdom of nature. Those of polished nations are ascribed to themselves, and are supposed to indicate a capacity superior to that of rude minds. But the establishments of men, like those of every animal, are suggested by nature, and are the result of instinct, directed by the variety of situations in which mankind are placed. Those establishments arose from successive improvements that were made, without any sense of their general effect; and they bring human affairs to a state of complication, which the greatest reach of capacity with which human nature was ever adorned, could not have projected; nor even when the whole is carried into execution, can it be comprehended in its full extent.

Who could anticipate, or even enumerate, the separate occupations and professions by which the members of any commercial state are distinguished; the variety of devices which are practiced in separate cells, and which the artist, attentive to his own affair, has invented, to abridge or to facilitate his separate task? In coming to this mighty end, every generation, compared to its predecessors, may have appeared to be ingenious; compared to its followers, may have appeared to be dull: and human ingenuity, whatever heights it may have gained in a succession of ages, continues to move with an equal pace, and to creep in making the last as well as the first step of commercial or civil improvement.

It may even be doubted, whether the measure of national capacity increases with the advancement of arts. Many mechanical arts, indeed, require no capacity; they succeed best under a total suppression of sentiment and reason; and ignorance is the mother of industry as well as of superstition. Reflection and fancy are subject to err; but a habit of moving the hand, or the foot, is independent of either. Manufactures, accordingly, prosper most, where the mind is least consulted, and where the workshop may, without any great effort of imagination, be considered as an engine, the parts of which are men.

The forest has been felled by the savage without the use of the axe, and weights have been raised without the aid of the mechanical powers. The merit of the inventor, in every branch, probably deserves a preference to that of the performer; and he who invented a tool, or could work without its assistance, deserved the praise of ingenuity in a much higher degree than the mere artist, who, by its assistance, produced a superior work.

But if many parts in the practice of every art, and in the detail of every department, require no abilities, or actually tend to contract and to limit the views of the mind, there are others which lead to general reflections, and to enlargement of thought. Even in manufacture, the genius of the master, perhaps, is cultivated, while that of the inferior workman lies waste. The statesman may have a wide comprehension of human affairs, while the tools he employs are ignorant of the system in which they are themselves combined. The general officer may be a great proficient in the knowledge of war, while the soldier is confined to a few motions of the hand and the foot. The former may have gained, what the latter has lost; and being occupied in the conduct of disciplined armies, may practice on a larger scale, all the arts of preservation, of deception, and of stratagem, which the savage exerts in leading a small party, or merely in defending himself.

The practitioner of every art and profession may afford matter of general speculation to the man of science; and thinking itself, in this age of separations, may become a peculiar craft. In the bustle of civil pursuits and occupations, men appear in a variety of lights, and suggest matter of inquiry and fancy, by which conversation is enlivened, and greatly enlarged. The productions of ingenuity are brought to the market; and men are willing to pay for whatever has a tendency to inform or amuse. By this means the idle, as well as the busy, contribute to forward the progress of arts, and bestow on polished nations that air of superior ingenuity, under which they appear to have gained the ends that were pursued by the savage in his forest, knowledge, order, and wealth.

PART V

SECTION III: Of Relaxations in the National Spirit incident to Polished Nations

...

We may fancy to ourselves, that in ages of progress, the human race, like scouts gone abroad on the discovery of fertile lands, having the world open before them, are presented at every step with the appearance of novelty. They enter on every new ground with expectation and joy: They engage in every enterprise with the ardour of men, who believe they are going to arrive at national felicity, and permanent glory; and forget past disappointments amidst the hopes of future success. From mere ignorance, rude minds are intoxicated with every passion; and partial to their own condition, and to their own pursuits, they think that every scene is inferior to that in which they are placed. Roused alike by success, and by misfortune, they are sanguine, ardent, and precipitant; and leave to the more knowing ages which succeed them, monuments of imperfect skill, and of rude execution in every art; but they leave likewise the marks of a vigorous and ardent spirit, which their successors are not always qualified to sustain, or to imitate.

This may be admitted, perhaps, as a fair description of prosperous societies, at least during certain periods of their progress. The spirit with which they advance may be unequal, in different ages, and may have its paroxysms, and intermissions, arising from the inconstancy of human passions, and from the casual appearance or removal of occasions that excite them. But does this spirit, which for a time continues to carry on the project of civil and commercial arts, find a natural pause in the termination of its own pursuits? May the business of civil society be accomplished, and may the occasion of farther exertion be removed? Do continued disappointments reduce sanguine hopes, and familiarity with objects blunt the edge of novelty? Does experience itself cool the ardour of the mind? May the society be again compared to the individual? And may it be suspected, although the vigour of a nation, like that of a natural body, does not waste by a physical decay, that yet it may sicken for want of exercise, and die in the close of its own exertions? May societies, in the completion of all their designs, like men in years, who disregard the amusements, and are insensible to the passions, of youth, become cold and indifferent to objects that used to animate in a ruder age? And may a polished community be compared to a man, who having executed his plan, built his house, and made his settlement; who having, in short, exhausted the charms of every subject, and wasted all his ardour, sinks into languor and listless indifference? If so, we have found at least another simile to our purpose. But it is probable, that here too, the resemblance is imperfect; and the inference that would follow, like that of most arguments drawn from analogy, tends rather to amuse the fancy, than to give any real information on the subject to which it refers.

The materials of human art are never entirely exhausted, and the applications of industry are never at an end. The national ardour is not, at any particular time, proportioned to the occasion there is for activity; nor curiosity, to the extent of subject that remains to be studied.

The ignorant and the artless, to whom objects of science are new, and who are worst furnished with the conveniences of life, instead of being more active, and more curious, are commonly more quiescent, and less inquisitive, than the knowing and the polished. When we compare the particulars which occupy mankind in their rude and in their polished condition, they will be found greatly multiplied and enlarged in the last. The questions we have put, however, deserve to be answered; and if, in the advanced ages of society, we do not find the objects of human pursuit removed, or greatly diminished, we may find them at least changed; and in estimating the national spirit, we may find a negligence in one part, but ill compensated by the growing attention which is paid to another.

It is true, in general, that in all our pursuits, there is a termination of trouble, and a point of repose to which we aspire. We would remove this inconvenience, or gain that advantage, that our labours may cease. When I have conquered Italy and Sicily, says Pyrrhus, I shall then enjoy my repose. This termination is proposed in our national as well as in our personal exertions; and in spite of frequent experience to the contrary, is considered at a distance as the height of felicity. But nature has wisely, in most particulars, baffled our project; and placed nowhere within our reach this visionary blessing of absolute ease. The attainment of one end is but the beginning of a new pursuit; and the discovery of one art is but a prolongation of the thread by which we are conducted to further inquiries, and only hope to escape from the labyrinth.

Among the occupations that may be enumerated, as tending to exercise the invention, and to cultivate the talents of men, are the pursuits of accommodation and wealth, including all the different contrivances which serve to increase manufactures, and to perfect the mechanical arts. But it must be owned, that as the materials of commerce may continue to be accumulated without any determinate limit, so the arts which are applied to improve them, may admit of perpetual refinements. No measure of fortune, or degree of skill, is found to diminish the supposed necessities of human life; refinement and plenty foster new desires, while they furnish the means, or practice the methods, to gratify them.

In the result of commercial arts, inequalities of fortune are greatly increased, and the majority of every people are obliged by necessity, or at least strongly incited by ambition and avarice, to employ every talent they possess. After a history of some thousand years employed in manufacture and commerce, the inhabitants of China are still the most laborious and industrious of any people on the surface of the earth.

Some part of this observation may be extended to the elegant and literary arts. They too have their materials, which cannot be exhausted, and proceed from desires which cannot be satiated. But the respect paid to literary merit is fluctuating, and matter of transient fashion. When learned productions accumulate, the acquisition of knowledge occupies the time that might be bestowed on invention. The object of mere learning is attained with moderate or inferior talents, and the growing list of pretenders diminishes the lustre of the few who are eminent. When we only mean to learn what others have taught, it is probable, that even our knowledge will be less than that of our masters. Great names continue to be repeated with admiration, after we have ceased to examine the foundations of our praise: and new pretenders are rejected, not because they fall short of their predecessors, but because they do not excel them; or because, in reality, we have, without examination, taken for granted the merit of the first, and cannot judge of either.

After libraries are furnished, and every path of ingenuity is occupied, we are, in proportion to our admiration of what is already done, prepossessed against farther attempts. We become students and admirers, instead of rivals; and substitute the knowledge of books, instead of the inquisitive or animated spirit in which they were written.

The commercial and lucrative arts may continue to prosper, but they gain an ascendant at the expense of other pursuits. The desire of profit stifles the love of perfection. Interest cools the imagination, and hardens the heart; and, recommending employments in proportion as they are lucrative, and certain in their gains, it drives ingenuity, and ambition itself, to the counter and the workshop.

But apart from these considerations, the separation of professions, while it seems to promise improvement of skill, and is actually the cause why the productions of every art become more perfect as commerce advances; yet in its termination, and ultimate effects, serves, in some measure, to break the bands of society, to substitute form in place of ingenuity, and to withdraw individuals from the common scene of occupation, on which the sentiments of the heart, and the mind, are most happily employed.

Under the *distinction* of callings, by which the members of polished society are separated from each other, every individual is supposed to possess his species of talent, or his peculiar skill, in which the others are confessedly ignorant; and society is made to consist of parts, of which none is animated with the spirit of society itself. "We see in the same persons", said Pericles, "an equal attention to private and to public affairs; and in men who have turned to separate professions, a competent knowledge of what relates to the community; for we alone consider those who are inattentive to the state, as perfectly insignificant". This encomium on the Athenians, was probably offered under an apprehension, that the contrary was likely to be charged by their enemies, or might soon take place. It happened accordingly, that the business of state, as well as of war, came to be worse administered at Athens, when these, as well as other applications, became the objects of separate professions; and the history of this people abundantly showed, that men ceased to be citizens, even to be good poets and orators, in proportion as they came to be distinguished by the profession of these, and other separate crafts.

Animals less honoured than we, have sagacity enough to procure their food, and to find the means of their solitary pleasures; but it is reserved for man to consult, to persuade, to oppose, to kindle in the society of his fellow-creatures, and to lose the sense of his personal interest or safety, in the ardour of his friendships and his oppositions.

When we are involved in any of the divisions into which mankind are separated, under the denominations of a country, a tribe, or an order of men any way affected by common interests, and guided by communicating passions, the mind recognises its natural station; the sentiments of the heart, and the talents of the understanding, find their natural exercise. Wisdom, vigilance, fidelity, and fortitude, are the characters requisite in such a scene, and the qualities which it tends to improve.

In simple or barbarous ages, when nations are weak, and beset with enemies, the love of a country, of a party, or a faction, are the same. The public is a knot of friends, and its enemies are the rest of mankind. Death or slavery are the ordinary evils which they are concerned to ward off; victory and dominion, the objects to which they aspire. Under the sense of what they may suffer from foreign invasions, it is one object, in every prosperous society, to increase its force, and to extend its limits. In proportion as this object is gained, security increases. They who possess the interior districts, remote from the frontier, are unused to alarms from abroad. They who are placed on the extremities, remote from the seats of government, are unused to hear of political interests; and the public becomes an object perhaps too extensive, for the conceptions of either. They enjoy the protection of its laws, or of its armies; and they boast of its splendour, and its power; but the glowing sentiments of public affection, which, in small states, mingle with the tenderness of the parent and the lover, of the friend and the companion, merely by having their object enlarged, lose great part of their force.

The manners of rude nations require to be reformed. Their foreign quarrels, and domestic dissensions, are the operations of extreme and sanguinary passions. A state of greater tranquility hath many happy effects. But if nations pursue the plan of enlargement and pacification, till their members can no longer apprehend the common ties of society, nor be engaged by affection in the cause of their country, they must err on the opposite side, and by leaving too little to agitate the spirits of men, bring on ages of languor, if not of decay.

The members of a community may, in this manner, like the inhabitants of a conquered province, be made to lose the sense of every connection, but that of kindred or neighbourhood; and have no common affairs to transact, but those of trade: Connections, indeed, or transactions, in which probity and friendship may still take place; but in which the national spirit, whose ebbs and flows we are now considering, cannot be exerted.

What we observe, however, on the tendency of enlargement to loosen the bands of political union, cannot be applied to nations who, being originally narrow, never greatly extended their limits, nor to those who, in a rude state, had already the extension of a great kingdom.

In territories of considerable extent, subject to one government, and possessed of freedom, the national union, in rude ages, is extremely imperfect. Every district forms a separate party; and the descendants of different families are opposed to one another, under the denomination of *tribes* or of *clans*: they are seldom brought to act with a steady concert; their feuds and animosities give more frequently the appearance of so many nations at war, than of a people united by connections of policy. They acquire a spirit, however, in their private divisions, and in the midst of a disorder, otherwise hurtful, of which the force, on many occasions, redounds to the power of the state.

Whatever be the national extent, civil order, and regular government, are advantages of the greatest importance; but it does not follow, that every arrangement made to obtain these ends, and which may, in the making, exercise and cultivate the best qualities of men, is therefore of a nature to produce permanent effects, and to secure the preservation of that national spirit from which it arose.

We have reason to dread the political refinements of ordinary men, when we consider, that repose, or inaction itself, is in a great measure their object; and that they would frequently model their governments, not merely to prevent injustice and error, but to prevent agitation and bustle; and by the barriers they raise against the evil actions of men, would prevent them from acting at all. Every dispute of a free people, in the opinion of such politicians, amounts to disorder, and a breach of the national peace. What heart-burnings? What delay to affairs? What want of secrecy and dispatch? What defect of police? Men of superior genius sometimes seem to imagine, that the vulgar have no title to act, or to think. A great prince is pleased to ridicule the precaution by which judges in a free country are confined to the strict interpretation of law.

We easily learn to contract our opinions of what men may, in consistence with public order, be safely permitted to do. The agitations of a republic, and the license of its members, strike the subjects of monarchy with aversion and disgust. The freedom with which the European is left to traverse the streets and the fields, would appear to a Chinese a sure prelude to confusion and anarchy. "Can men behold their superior and not tremble? Can they converse without a precise and written ceremonial? What hopes of peace, if the streets are not barricaded at an hour? What wild disorder, if men are permitted in any thing to do what they please?"

If the precautions which men thus take against each other be necessary to repress their crimes, and do not arise from a corrupt ambition, or from cruel jealousy in their rulers, the proceeding itself must be applauded, as the best remedy of which the vices of men will admit. The viper must be held at a distance, and the tiger chained. But if a rigorous policy, applied to enslave, not to restrain from crimes, has an actual tendency to corrupt the manners, and to extinguish the spirit of nations; if its severities be applied to terminate the agitations of a free people, not to remedy their corruptions; if forms be often applauded as salutary, because they tend merely to silence the voice of mankind, or be condemned as pernicious, because they allow this voice to be heard; we may expect that many of the boasted improvements of civil society, will be mere devices to lay the political spirit at rest, and will chain up the active virtues more than the restless disorders of men.

If to any people it be the avowed object of policy, in all its internal refinements, to secure the person and the property of the subject, without any regard to his political character, the constitution indeed may be free, but its members may likewise become unworthy of the freedom they possess, and unfit to preserve it. The effects of such a constitution may be to immerse all orders of men in their separate pursuits of pleasure, which they may now enjoy with little disturbance; or of gain, which they may preserve without any attention to the commonwealth.

If this be the end of political struggles, the design, when executed, in securing to the individual his estate, and the means of subsistence, may put an end to the exercise of those very virtues that were required in conducting its execution. A man who, in concert with his fellow-subjects, contends with usurpation in defense of his estate or his person, may find an exertion of great generosity, and of a vigorous spirit; but he who, under political establishments, supposed to be fully confirmed, betakes him, because he is safe, to the mere enjoyment of fortune, has in fact turned to a source of corruption the very advantages which the virtues of the other procured. Individuals, in certain ages, derive their protection chiefly from the strength of the party to which they adhere; but in times of corruption, they flatter themselves, that they may continue to derive from the public that safety which, in former ages, they must have owed to their own vigilance and spirit, to the warm attachment of their friends, and to the exercise of every talent which could render them respected, feared, or beloved. In one period, therefore, mere circumstances serve to excite the spirit, and to preserve the manners of men; in another, great wisdom and zeal for the good of mankind on the part of their leaders, are required for the same purposes.

Rome, it may be thought, did not die of lethargy, nor perish by the remission of her political ardours at home. Her distemper appeared of a nature more violent and acute. Yet if the virtues of Cato and of Brutus found an exercise in the dying hour of the republic, the neutrality, and the cautious retirement of Atticus, found its security in the same tempestuous season; and the great body of the people lay undisturbed, below the current of a storm, by which the superior ranks of men were destroyed. In the minds of the people, the sense of a public was defaced; and even the animosity of faction had subsided: they only could share in the commotion, who were the soldiers of a legion, or the partisans of a leader. But this state fell not into obscurity for want of eminent men. If at the time of which we speak, we look only for a few names distinguished in the history of mankind, there is no period at which the list was more numerous. But those names became distinguished in the contest for dominion, not in the exercise of equal rights: the people were corrupted; the empire of the known world stood in need of a master.

Republican governments, in general, are in hazard of ruin from the ascendant of particular factions, and from the mutinous spirit of a populace, who being corrupted, are no longer fit to share in the administration of state. But under other establishments, where liberty may be more successfully attained if men are corrupted, the national vigour declines from the abuse of that very security which is procured by the supposed perfection of public order.

A distribution of power and office; an execution of law, by which mutual encroachments and molestations are brought to an end; by which the person and the property are, without friends, without cabal, without obligation, perfectly secured to individuals, does honour to the genius of a nation; and could not have been fully established, without those exertions of understanding and integrity, those trials of a resolute and vigorous spirit, which adorn the annals of a people, and leave to future ages a subject of just admiration and applause. But if we suppose that the end is attained, and that men no longer act, in the enjoyment of liberty, from liberal sentiments, or with a view to the preservation of public manners; if individuals think themselves secure without any attention or effort of their own; this boasted advantage may be found only to give them an opportunity of enjoying, at leisure, the conveniences and necessaries of life; or, in the language of Cato, teach them to value their houses, their villas, their statues, and their pictures, at a higher rate than they do the republic. They may be found to grow tired in secret of a free constitution, of which they never cease to boast in their conversation, and which they always neglect in their conduct.

The dangers to liberty are not the subject of our present consideration; but they can never be greater from any cause than they are from the supposed remissness of a people, to whose personal vigour every constitution, as it owed its establishment, so must continue to owe its preservation. Nor is this blessing ever less secure than it is in the possession of men who think that they enjoy it in safety, and who therefore consider the public only as it presents to their avarice a number of lucrative employments; for the sake of which they may sacrifice those very rights which render themselves objects of management or consideration.

From the tendency of these reflections, then, it should appear, that a national spirit is frequently transient, not on account of any incurable distemper in the nature of mankind, but on account of their voluntary neglects and corruptions. This spirit subsisted solely, perhaps, in the execution of a few projects, entered into for the acquisition of territory or wealth; it comes, like a useless weapon, to be laid aside after its end is attained.

Ordinary establishments terminate in a relaxation of vigour, and are ineffectual to the preservation of states; because they lead mankind to rely on their arts, instead of their virtues, and to mistake for an improvement of human nature, a mere accession of accommodation, or of riches. Institutions that fortify the mind, inspire courage, and promote national felicity, can never tend to national ruin.

Is it not possible, amidst our admiration of arts, to find some place for these? Let statesmen, who are entrusted with the government of nations, reply for themselves. It is their business to show, whether they climb into stations of eminence, merely to display a passion for interest, which they had better indulge in obscurity; and whether they have capacity to understand the happiness of a people, the conduct of whose affairs they are so willing to undertake.

SECTION IV: The same subject continued

Men frequently, while they study to improve their fortunes, neglect themselves; and while they reason for their country, forget the considerations that most deserve their attention. Numbers, riches, and the other resources of war, are highly important: but nations consist of men; and a nation consisting of degenerate and cowardly men, is weak; a nation consisting of vigorous, public-spirited, and resolute men, is strong. The resources of war, where other advantages are equal, may decide a contest; but the resources of war, in hands that cannot employ them, are of no avail.

Virtue is a necessary constituent of national strength: capacity, and a vigorous understanding, are no less necessary to sustain the fortune of states. Both are improved by discipline, and by the exercises in which men are engaged. We despise, or we pity, the lot of mankind, while they lived under uncertain establishments, and were obliged to sustain in the same person, the character of the senator, the statesman, and the soldier. Polished nations discover, that anyone of these characters is sufficient in one person; and that the ends of each, when disjoined, are more easily accomplished. The first, however, were circumstances under which nations advanced and prospered; the second were those in which the spirit relaxed, and the nation went to decay.

We may, with good reason, congratulate our species on their having escaped from a state of barbarous disorder and violence, into a state of domestic peace and regular policy; when they have sheathed the dagger, and disarmed the animosities of civil contention; when the weapons with which they contend are the reasonings of the wise, and the tongue of the eloquent. But we cannot, mean-time, help to regret, that they should ever proceed, in search of perfection, to place every branch of administration behind the counter, and come to employ, instead of the statesman and warrior, the mere clerk and accountant.

By carrying this system to its height, men are educated, who could copy for Caesar his military instructions, or even execute a part of his plans; but none who could act in all the different scenes for which the leader himself must be qualified, in the state and in the field, in times of order or of tumult, in times of division or of unanimity; none who could animate the council when deliberating on ordinary occasions, or when alarmed by attacks from abroad.

The policy of China is the most perfect model of an arrangement, at which the ordinary refinements of government are aimed; and the inhabitants of this empire possess, in the highest degree, those arts on which vulgar minds make the felicity and greatness of nations to depend. The state has acquired, in a measure unequalled in the history of mankind, numbers of men, and the other resources of war. They have done what we are very apt to admire; they have brought national affairs to the level of the meanest capacity; they have broke them into parts, and thrown them into separate departments; they have clothed every proceeding with splendid ceremonies, and majestical forms; and where the reverence of forms cannot repress disorder, a rigorous and severe police, armed with every species of corporal punishment, is applied to the purpose. The whip, and the cudgel, are held up to all orders of men; they are at once employed, and they are dreaded by every magistrate. A mandarine is whipped, for having ordered a pickpocket to receive too few or too many blows.

Every department of state is made the object of a separate profession, and every candidate for office must have passed through a regular education; and, as in the graduations of the university, must have obtained by his proficiency, or his standing, the degree to which he aspires. The tribunals of state, of war, and of the revenue, as well as of literature, are conducted by graduates in their different studies: but while learning is the great road to preferment, it terminates, in being able to read, and to write; and the great object of government consists in raising, and in consuming the fruits of the earth. With all these resources, and this learned preparation, which is made to turn these resources to use, the state is in reality weak; has repeatedly given the example which we seek to explain; and among the doctors of war or of policy, among the millions who are set apart for the military profession, can find none of its members who are fit to stand forth in the dangers of their country, or to form a defense against the repeated inroads of an enemy reputed to be artless and mean.

It is difficult to tell how long the decay of states might be suspended by the cultivation of arts on which their real felicity and strength depend; by cultivating in the higher ranks those talents for the council and the field, which cannot, without great disadvantage, be separated; and in the body of a people, that zeal for their country, and that military character, which enable them to take a share in defending its rights.

Times may come, when every proprietor must defend his own possessions, and every free people maintain their own independence. We may imagine, that against such an extremity, an army of hired troops is a sufficient precaution; but their own troops are the very enemy against which a people is sometimes obliged to fight. We may flatter ourselves, that extremities of this sort, in any particular case, are remote; but we cannot, in reasoning on the general fortunes of mankind, avoid putting the case, and referring to the examples in which it has happened. It has happened in every instance where the polished have fallen a prey to the rude, and where the pacific inhabitant has been reduced to subjection by military force.

If the defense and government of a people be made to depend on a few, who make the conduct of state or of war their profession; whether these be foreigners or natives; whether they be called away of a sudden, like the Roman legion from Britain; whether they turn against their employers, like the army of Carthage, or be overpowered and dispersed by a stroke of fortune, the multitude of a cowardly and undisciplined people must, on such an emergence, receive a foreign or a domestic enemy, as they would a plague or an earthquake, with hopeless amazement and terror, and by their numbers, only swell the triumphs, and enrich the spoil of a conqueror.

Statesmen and leaders of armies, accustomed to the mere observance of forms, are disconcerted by a suspension of customary rules; and on sight grounds despair of their country. They were qualified only to go the rounds of a particular track; and when forced from their stations, are in reality unable to act with men. They only took part in formalities, of which they understood not the tendency; and together with the modes of procedure, even the very state itself, in their apprehension, has ceased to exist. The numbers, possessions, and resources of a great people, only serve, in their view, to constitute a scene of hopeless confusion and terror.

In rude ages, under the appellations of *a community, a people,* or *a nation,* was understood a number of men; and the state, while its members remained, was accounted entire. The Scythians, while they fled before Darius, mocked at his childish attempt; Athens survived the devastations of Xerxes; and Rome, in its rude state, those of the Gauls. With polished and mercantile states, the case is sometimes reversed. The nation is a territory, cultivated and improved by its owners; destroy the possession, even while the master remains, the state is undone.

That weakness and effeminacy of which polished nations are sometimes accused, has its place probably in the mind alone. The strength of animals, and that of man in particular, depends on his feeding, and the kind of labour to which he is used. Wholesome food, and hard labour, the portion of many in every polished and commercial nation, secure to the public a number of men endued with bodily strength, and inured to hardship and toil.

Even delicate living, and good accommodation, are not found to enervate the body. The armies of Europe have been obliged to make the experiment; and the children of opulent families, bred in effeminacy, or nursed with tender care, have been made to contend with the savage. By imitating his arts, they have learned, like him, to traverse the forest; and, in every season, to subsist in the desert. They have, perhaps, recovered a lesson, which it has cost civilized nations many ages to unlearn, That the fortune of a man is entire while he remains possessed of himself.

It may be thought, however, that few of the celebrated nations of antiquity, whose fate has given rise to so much reflection on the vicissitudes of human affairs, had made any great progress in those enervating arts we have mentioned; or made those arrangements from which the danger in question could be supposed to arise. The Greeks, in particular, at the time of their fall under the Macedonian yoke, had certainly not carried the commercial arts to so great a height as is common with the most flourishing and prosperous nations of Europe. They had still retained the form of independent republics; the people were generally admitted to a share in the government; and not being able to hire armies, they were obliged, by necessity, to bear a part in the defense of their country. By their frequent wars and domestic commotions, they were accustomed to danger, and were familiar with alarming situations: they were accordingly still accounted the best soldiers and the best statesmen of the known world. The younger Cyrus promised himself the empire of Asia by means of their aid; and after his fall, a body of ten thousand, although bereft of their leaders, baffled, in their retreat, all the military force of the Persian empire. The victor of Asia did not think himself prepared for that conquest, till he had formed an army from the subdued republics of Greece.

It is, however, true, that in the age of Philip, the military and political spirit of those nations appears to have been considerably impaired, and to have suffered, perhaps, from the variety of interests and pursuits, as well as of pleasures, with which their members came to be occupied: they even made a kind of separation between the civil and military character. Phocion, we are told by Plutarch, having observed that the leading men of his time followed different courses, that some applied themselves to civil, others to military affairs, determined rather to follow the examples of Themistocles, Aristides, and Pericles, the leaders of a former age, who were equally prepared for either.

We find in the orations of Demosthenes, a perpetual reference to this state of manners. We find him exhorting the Athenians, not only to declare war, but to arm themselves for the execution of their own military plans. We find that there was an order of military men, who easily passed from the service of one state to that of another; and who, when they were neglected from home, turned away to enterprises on their own account. There were not, perhaps, better warriors in any former age; but those warriors were not attached to any state; and the settled inhabitants of every city thought themselves disqualified for military service. The discipline of armies was perhaps improved; but the vigour of nations was gone to decay. When Philip, or Alexander, defeated the Grecian armies, which were chiefly composed of soldiers of fortune, they found an easy conquest with the other inhabitants: and when the latter, afterwards supported by those soldiers, invaded the Persian empire, he seems to have left little martial spirit behind him; and by removing the military men, to have taken precaution enough, in his absence, to secure his dominion over this mutinous and refractory people.

The subdivision of arts and professions, in certain examples, tends to improve the practice of them, and to promote their ends. By having separated the arts of the clothier and the tanner, we are the better supplied with shoes and with cloth. But to separate the arts which form the citizen and the statesman, the arts of policy and war, is an attempt to dismember the human character, and to destroy those very arts we mean to improve. By this separation, we in effect deprive a free people of what is necessary to their safety; or we prepare a defense against invasions from abroad, which gives a prospect of usurpation, and threatens the establishment of military government at home.

We may be surprised to find the beginning of certain military instructions at Rome, referred to a time no earlier than that of the Cimbric war. It was then, we are told by Valerius Maximus, that Roman soldiers were made to learn from gladiators the use of a sword: and the antagonists of Phyrrhus and of Hannibal were, by the account of this writer, still in need of instruction in the first rudiments of their trade. They had already, by the order and choice of their encampments, impressed the Grecian invader with awe and respect; they had already, not by their victories, but by their national vigour and firmness, under repeated defeats, induced him to sue for peace. But the haughty Roman, perhaps, knew the advantage of order and of union, without having been broke to the inferior arts of the mercenary soldier; and had the courage to face the enemies of his country, without having practiced the use of his weapon under the fear of being whipped. He could still be persuaded, that a time might come, when refined and intelligent nations would make the art of war to consist in a few technical forms, that citizens and soldiers might come to be distinguished as much as women and men; that the citizen would become possessed of a property which he would not be able, or required, to defend; that the soldier would be appointed to keep for another what he would be taught to desire, and what he would be enabled to seize for himself; that, in short, one set of men were to have an interest in the preservation of civil establishments, without the power to defend them; that the other were to have this power, without either the inclination or the interest.

This people, however, by degrees came to put their military force on the very footing to which this description alludes. Marius made a capital change in the manner of levying soldiers at Rome: He filled his legions with the mean and the indigent, who depended on military pay for subsistence; he created a force which rested on mere discipline alone, and the skill of the gladiator; he taught his troops to employ their swords against the constitution of their country, and set the example of a practice which was soon adopted and improved by his successors.

The Romans only meant by their armies to encroach on the freedom of other nations, while they preserved their own. They forgot, that in assembling soldiers of fortune, and in suffering any leader to be master of a disciplined army, they actually resigned their political rights, and suffered a master to arise for the state. This people, in short, whose ruling passion was depredation and conquest, perished by the recoil of an engine which they themselves had erected against mankind.

The boasted refinements, then, of the polished age, are not divested of danger. They open a door, perhaps, to disaster, as wide and accessible as any of those they have shut. If they build walls and ramparts, they enervate the minds of those who are placed to defend them; if they form disciplined armies, they reduce the military spirit of entire nations; and by placing the sword where they have given a distaste to civil establishments, they prepare for mankind the government of force.

It is happy for the nations of Europe, that the disparity between the soldier and the pacific citizen can never be so great as it became among the Greeks and the Romans. In the use of modern arms, the novice is made to learn, and to practice with ease, all that the veteran knows; and if to teach him were a matter of real difficulty, happy are they who are not deterred by such difficulties, and who can discover the arts which tend to fortify and preserve, not to enervate and ruin their country.

SECTION V: Of National Waste

The strength of nations consists in the wealth, the numbers, and the character, of their people. The history of their progress from a state of rudeness, is, for the most part, a detail of the struggles they have maintained, and of the arts they have practiced, to strengthen, or to secure themselves. Their conquests, their population, and their commerce, their civil and military arrangements, their skill in the construction of weapons, and in the methods of attack and defense; the very distribution of tasks, whether in private business or in public affairs, either tend to bestow, or promise to employ with advantage, the constituents of a national force, and the resources of war.

If we suppose, that together with these advantages, the military character of a people remains, or is improved, it must follow, that what is gained in civilization, is a real increase of strength; and that the ruin of nations could never take its rise from themselves. Where states have stopped short in their progress, or have actually gone to decay, we may suspect, that however disposed to advance, they have found a limit, beyond which they could not proceed; or from a remission of the national spirit, and a weakness of character, were unable to make the most of their resources, and natural advantages. On this supposition, from being stationary, they may begin to relapse, and by a retrograde motion, in a succession of ages, arrive at a state of greater weakness, than that which they quitted in the beginning of their progress; and with the appearance of better arts, and superior conduct, expose themselves to become a prey to barbarians, whom, in the attainment, or the height of their glory, they had easily baffled or despised.

Whatever may be the natural wealth of a people, or whatever may be the limits beyond which they cannot improve on their stock, it is probable, that no nation has ever reached those limits, or has been able to postpone its misfortunes, and the effects of misconduct, until its fund of materials, and the fertility of its soil, were exhausted, or the numbers of its people were greatly reduced. The same errors in policy, and weakness of manners, which prevent the proper use of resources, likewise check their increase, or improvement.

The wealth of the state consists in the fortune of its members. The actual revenue of the state is that share of every private fortune, which the public has been accustomed to demand for national purposes. This revenue cannot be always proportioned to what may be supposed redundant in the private estate, but to what is, in some measure, thought so by the owner; and to what he may be made to spare, without entrenching on his manner of living, and without suspending his projects of expense, or of commerce. It should appear, therefore, that any immoderate increase of private expense is a prelude to national weakness: government, even while each of its subjects consumes a princely estate, may be straitened in point of revenue, and the paradox be explained by example, That the public is poor, while its members are rich.

We are frequently led into error by mistaking money for riches; we think that a people cannot be impoverished by a waste of money which is spent among themselves. The fact is, that men are impoverished, only in two ways; either by having their gains suspended, or by having their substance consumed; and money expended at home, being circulated, and not consumed, cannot, any more than the exchange of a tally, or a counter, among a certain number of hands, tend to diminish the wealth of the company among whom it is handed about. But while money circulates at home, the necessaries of life, which are the real constituents of wealth, may be idly consumed; the industry which might be employed to increase the stock of a people, may be suspended, or turned to abuse.

Great armies, maintained either at home or abroad, without any national object, are so many mouths unnecessarily opened to waste the stores of the public, and so many hands with-held from the arts by which its profits are made. Unsuccessful enterprises are so many ventures thrown away, and losses sustained, proportioned to the capital employed in the service. The Helvetii, in order to invade the Roman province of Gaul, burnt their habitations, dropt their instruments of husbandry, and consumed, in one year, the savings of many. The enterprise failed of success, and the nation was undone.

States have endeavoured, in some instances, by pawning their credit, instead of employing their capital, to disguise the hazards they ran. They have found, in the loans they raised, a casual resource, which encouraged their enterprises. They have seemed, by their manner of erecting transferable funds, to leave the capital for purposes of trade, in the hands of the subject, while it is actually expended by the government. They have, by these means, proceeded to the execution of great national projects, without suspending private industry, and have left future ages to answer, in part, for debts contracted with a view to future emolument. So far the expedient is plausible, and appears to be just. The growing burden too, is thus gradually laid; and if a nation be to sink in some future age, every minister hopes it may still keep afloat in his own. But the measure, for this very reason, is, with all its advantages, extremely dangerous, in the hands of a precipitant and ambitious administration, regarding only the present occasion, and imagining a state to be inexhaustible, while a capital can be borrowed, and the interest be paid.

We are told of a nation, who, during a certain period, rivalled the glories of the ancient world, threw off the dominion of a master armed against them with the powers of a great kingdom, broke the yoke with which they had been oppressed, and almost within the course of a century, raised, by their industry and national vigour, a new and formidable power, which struck the former potentates of Europe with awe and suspense, and turned the badges of poverty with which they set out, into the ensigns of war and dominion. This end was attained by the great efforts of a spirit awaked by oppression, by a successful pursuit of national wealth, and by a rapid anticipation of future revenue. But this illustrious state is supposed, not only in the language of a former section, to have preoccupied the business; they have sequestered the inheritance of many ages to come.

Great national expense, however, does not imply the necessity of any national suffering. While revenue is applied with success, to obtain some valuable end; the profits of every adventure, being more than sufficient to repay its costs, the public should gain, and its resources should continue to multiply. But an expense, whether sustained at home or abroad, whether a waste of the present, or an anticipation of future, revenue, if it bring no proper return, is to be reckoned among the causes of national ruin.

ID. Utopian Imagination
& Radical Reforms

Five
Robert Wallace
(1697–1771)

VARIOUS PROSPECTS ON MANKIND, NATURE AND PROVIDENCE (1761)

PROSPECT II.

The model of a perfect Government, not for a single Nation only, but for the whole Earth.

As mankind can neither purchase nor secure what is necessary for their comfortable subsistence without society, so society cannot long continue peaceable and stable without civil government. We may therefore conclude, that government took place very early; and this is confirmed by the most ancient remains of history and tradition.

...

Besides such forms of government as have been actually established, many models have been proposed, which have only existed in the imagination of their projectors: of these the Commonwealth of Plato, the Utopia of Sir Thomas More, and Harrington's Oceana, are the most celebrated, and contain many ingenious observations and useful hints. The fancy of forming new plans of government has not entirely ceased. The ingenious Mr. Hume has very lately given us his idea of a perfect commonwealth among the rest of his political discourses. There is still room for further trials of this kind. The subject will not be easily exhausted. Old plans may be corrected, and experience may make the world wiser. Why therefore may not a new plan be proposed, especially if it aims at something greater, and can be made more comprehensive than any of the preceding, not being calculated for regulating the affairs of a single people, but for uniting all mankind under governments which shall preserve the same language, maintain an universal correspondence among the most distant inhabitants of the globe, and raise the whole human race to the highest perfection? Let us not immediately take it for granted, that such a government is utterly impracticable. Let us suspend our judgment till once we have considered whether we can conceive a consistent idea of it. After this it will be time enough to pronounce it impossible. This Prospect exhibits a sketch of such a happy constitution.

As it is absurd to suppose that mankind never had a beginning, let us imagine, that soon after their first appearance on our globe, when they amounted only to a thousand or ten thousand, or some such small number, they had been formed into a society in which there was to be no property, nor any division of lands for private use; but in place of establishing property, that they had agreed upon a proper and equitable distribution of the labour necessary for cultivating and adorning that spot of earth which they inhabited, and for supporting the whole society in common in an agreeable way. Let us suppose further, that the whole race of mankind who were alive at that time, and were then to be united in one society, had occupied a certain part of the earth consisting of ten thousand or a hundred thousand acres, or any other quantity, greater or less, proportionate to their number; or that they had measured out a tract of land according to the nature of the soil, or the natural division of the earth by seas, great rivers, or mountains. Suppose this territory to have been able to support a greater number, call it ten times, or a hundred times as many as were in the society when it was first erected. Suppose a regular plan to have been formed of the manner in which this tract of land was to be cultivated and adorned in the best manner, pointing out the situation of the houses, the manner of their architecture and different apartments, with their proper furniture; the methods of laying out the adjacent fields, sowing and planting them with all proper grains, herbs and trees, and storing them with cattle. Suppose this plan to have been as convenient, elegant, magnificent, as the society in these circumstances could be supposed capable of contriving and executing, with the art and skill of which they were masters, or with which the All-wise saw it proper to inspire them, in order to lay a foundation for the happy government of mankind in after ages. Suppose that this plan was to be carried into execution by all the members of the society, in such sort that none of them should be idle, or wholly exempted from working, nor should any be overburdened, or obliged to such hard and severe labour as might be prejudicial to their health, or indispose them for study and contemplation at proper seasons. Suppose all the members of the society to be executing this plan so as never to want, or to be in danger of wanting abundance of provisions of all kinds for their present comfortable subsistence, while they were gradually carrying on such works as were intended for ornament and magnificence, as well as for use. In a word, let us suppose this society to lay down proper rules for improving their minds in knowledge and virtue, and in this view to oblige their members to work only three or six hours a day, or in a greater or less proportion according to the exigencies of the society, leaving the rest of the time to be employed in study and contemplation, or in diversions and recreations of any kind, according to every man's humour, or agreeably to some particular rules and statutes consistent with the fundamental maxims of the government.

This is a first draught, or a general sketch of a more perfect constitution than has ever been established among any people.

On this subject one might easily go into a detail, and trace out many particular laws proper for such a society.

I   That some must be chosen to govern, that is, to take care that each of the members be employed in his proper work, and that none transgress the rules of the society.

II   That these governors should be very few in number.

III   That they should not be distinguished from the rest of the society by the elegance or magnificence of their clothes, houses or tables, but only by a simple badge of their office, without any ornament; as every other member of the society was to have a particular badge of his trade, of the same simple kind.

IV   That these governors were not usually to employ more hours in the oversight of the society than others did in their daily labours.

V   That care should be taken to have always a sufficient number of workmen and artists for the uses of the society, as masons, wrights, weavers, smiths, shoemakers, painters, musicians, statuaries, engravers, and all other persons proper for procuring not only the necessaries of life, but whatever was elegant and magnificent, if it was not fantastic, but agreeable to nature.

VI That a council should be appointed for assigning proper trades or employments to each boy and girl at a certain time of life, unless it might be thought more proper to leave every one to their own choice, or to the direction of their parents, without any interposition by the government, except upon some extraordinary occasions.

VII That in appointing proper trades to all in the society, whether men or women, regard should be had both to the strength of their bodies, and to their particular geniuses and dispositions of mind, as far as they could be discovered.

VIII That all sorts of useful labour should be honoured, and none of them should be treated with contempt.

IX That all the males, without exception, should be taught all the parts of agriculture, that every one might be able to give his assistance in seed-time and harvest, and no time might be lost whenever the season proved favourable.

X That great care should be taken of gardening, pasturage, and fishing.

XI That hunting and fowling should not be neglected.

XII That the members of the society should neither be distinguished by their houses, clothes, nor food, but all of them should enjoy every thing in the same manner, unless where particular distinctions must necessarily arise from differences in the soil, climate, or other circumstances, which rendered a variety proper or unavoidable.

XIII That there should be masters or teachers of all the particular arts and sciences, to instruct the children at those hours in which the rest of the society were employed in their different kinds of labour.

XIV That every man should be married between twenty four and twenty six years of age, or within a limited time, according to the nature of the climate, unless he could show a good reason to the contrary before a council appointed to take cognizance of such cases.

XV That no woman should be married before twenty years of age, or before a certain period suitable to the climate.

XVI   That while a woman was bearing children she should be obliged to no other work than nursing and taking care of them.

XVII That proper rules should be laid down for taking care of the sick and infirm, and for discharging the aged from all obligation to labour.

XVIII That there should be proper times for divine service, and proper persons appointed to preside in it, and to give lectures on piety and morality for the comfort and instruction of the people.

It is not necessary to enter upon a more minute detail of particular rules, as every one, either from this short sketch, or from Sir Thomas More's Utopia, may form a thousand constitutions consistent with the fundamental maxims of the society, of which this may be represented as the sum: "That there should be no private property. That every one should work for the public, and be supported by the public. That all should be on a level, and that the fruits of every one's labour should be common for the comfortable subsistence of all the members of the society. And, lastly, that every one should be obliged to do something, yet none should be burdened with severe labour."

As long as mankind live in peace and a good correspondence, and have abundance of room and provisions, they will increase and multiply. Under a government framed according to the preceding model, they must multiply much faster than under the happiest government that ever was actually established. Let us therefore suppose them increasing till the tract of earth which they had at first laid out for a habitation, though cultivated in the best manner, could no longer support them. Upon this they might make choice of another tract of land greater or less, as they found it convenient, or according to the natural division of the earth by seas, rivers, or mountains. This second territory they might people with a numerous a colony as they pleased, establishing a government founded on the same equitable maxims with the former. When this new government was fully peopled, there would be nothing to hinder them from founding a third and a fourth, and from going on continually in erecting new societies as often as they found it necessary or expedient.

In founding those new governments care might be taken,

1. That they should neither be too small nor too great. Perhaps fifty or a hundred miles in diameter, might be a sufficient extent, with an elegant and magnificent city near the center, from which noble roads should extend in straight lines to the extremity of that jurisdiction, with pleasant villages situated near the roads and all over the fields.
2. These different governments might either be of the same or of a different extent, as should be found most convenient.
3. Such governments might be erected, not only when the old were in danger of being overstocked, bud also on other occasions, and might either be settled in the neighbourhood of the more ancient governments, or at a greater distance, as might be judged most proper.
4. Such new colonies might be formed with such a various mixture of people from the old, that a regular and good correspondence, as well as the same language, might be perpetually preserved.
5. In order to strengthen this good correspondence, a plan might be devised for a regular migration of inhabitants from one climate to another, not only without any inconvenience, but to the great pleasure and profit of the citizens.

I need not go further into a detail; what is already observed is sufficient to give an idea of the whole. These are the outlines which might be filled up in a thousand different methods.

Whatever objections may be raised against a plan of this nature, it cannot be denied, that such a government is very proper for mankind, considered as rational animals. In entering into society such animals ought not only to provide for their mutual necessities, for their mutual security, and for the enjoyment of the pleasures which flow from fellowship and friendship, but should have a view to their mutual improvements and more speedy advances in useful arts and sciences. Clear and extensive knowledge is the glory of men as rational creatures. The labour of animals is not only necessary for procuring food and other conveniences, but also for preserving health, and for keeping the animal economy in vigour and repair. Mankind cannot cultivate the earth to so great advantage separately, as by their joint labours. Knowledge is most successfully acquired by unified endeavours. In modeling society, regard ought to be had to all these ends: labour ought not to be so fatiguing, or of so long continuance, as to weaken the body, or to destroy a taste for knowledge; or to leave no time, nor to give proper opportunities for acquiring it; but ought to be so equitably divided among all the members of the society, that no particular person may be overburdened, and that every one may both have time and proper means for acquiring knowledge.

How defective are all the plans of government which have ever been actually established! How miserably has the good end of government been defeated! How little care has been taken either of the souls or of the bodies of men! What are great numbers of the poor but slaves and beasts of burden to the rich! In what ignorance do multitudes live! To what severe labours are they subjected! How hard do they toil, yet how scanty and unwholesome is their diet! In what nasty cottages do they live! How few of the comforts of life fall to their share! How many have died by hunger and painful diseases, being cruelly neglected by their fellow creatures! Yet all these unhappy mortals were as much qualified by nature as the most fortunate of their kind, for a more agreeable life and nobler enjoyments. What government so fit for men, as that which equally provides for the happiness and improvement of the whole species?

PROSPECT III.

Whether Government, according to the preceding Model, ever could have been, or ever can be established and maintained in the World.

While my readers have been amusing themselves with the preceding sketch of human society, some of them, no doubt, have been tempted to laugh at my simplicity in taking any trouble to adjust systems of this nature... It will not, however, be disagreeable nor unprofitable to take a nearer view, and to consider,

I. Whether it was possible, at the beginning of the world, or in any period since the beginning; whether it is possible at this time, or ever will be possible, to establish such a government and education?

II. Supposing such a government once to be established, whether it could be preserved during any considerable length of time?

If we give credit to ancient historians, Lycurgus persuaded the Lacedemonians to agree to something of this kind, for they suffered their whole lands in Laconia, except such as belonged to the citizens of Sparta, to be divided into 30,000; and those which belonged to Sparta into 9,000; or as others say into 6,000, or according to a third party info 4,500 equal shares, and allotted them to a proportionable number of their citizens. I shall not call in question a history delivered down from the ancients with such solemnity. We ought not always to measure ancient by modern nations. But supposing the fact to be true, it is certain that the circumstances of that country in the age of Lycurgus, must have been very different from the circumstances of civilized nations in our age. It would be impossible at present to persuade any civilized nation whatsoever to agree to such a distribution. The rich and powerful part of the people have too many advantages above others ever to part with them, and put themselves on a level with their inferiors. In truth, no such generosity nor self-denial can be expected, nor ought to be demanded. Different maxims of government, different customs and notions are too deeply rooted ever to be eradicated in any ordinary way. One would be a madman to attempt it. Though Lycurgus and Solon, Plato and Aristotle, Demosthenes and Cicero, Sir Thomas More and Harrington, with all the ancient and modern philosophers, law-givers and orators, were to appear together, and endeavour to persuade the inhabitants of Great Britain, or France, to establish such a government, their efforts would be in vain. In order to bring about such a grand revolution, there would be a necessity for real miracles and inspiration, or for pretences to them, in imitation of Lycurgus, Minos and Numa; or at least for such a high strain of patriotism or enthusiasm as cannot reasonably be expected. If any such equal government is possible at present, according to the ordinary course of affairs, it must be erected in some wild and uncultivated country, where there are few inhabitants. This observation may be applied to all the ancient ages and nations; for it must have been extremely difficult to erect such a government in any ancient nation after the maxims which are contrary to the genius of it had prevailed widely, and taken firm root in the minds of men.

Neither could such a government have been erected at the beginning of the world without a miracle. This will be found to be equally true, whatever system we follow concerning the original of human affairs...

Abstracting from divine revelation we must have very imperfect conceptions of the first state of mankind, and of the time when, and the manner in which vice entered into the world. But whatever high notions we may form of men's innocence and purity at first; experience teaches us that they degenerated afterwards. Whether therefore, an idea of civil government was conceived in what may be called a state of innocence, or afterwards, it must have been imperfect at first. If before the depravity of mankind, the original plan could not fully answer in a state vicious and depraved; if after their innocence had been corrupted, many weak end wrong maxims must have been introduced, and have taken such firm root as would have rendered a perfect government altogether impracticable, till mankind by slow degrees, and after many trials, were taught by their experience, and by feeling the defects of their imperfect plans, were naturally led to a more perfect constitution.

Thus it appears, that a perfect government founded on equality, could not have been established at the beginning of the world, without a miracle.

It may, however, be allowed, if any such thing ever existed as that *state of nature* which some poets and philosophers have imagined, when men like other animals ranged through the fields without civil government; that, at the expiration of this state, mankind, instead of appropriating particular possessions to individuals, might have been led, by some lucky accidents, to have established societies, on the foundation of an original contract, mutually to assist and defend each particular member, in labouring for the general good of the community, in order to share mutually in the profits of every one's labour, and that such societies, though rude and imperfect at the beginning, might have laid the foundation of governments similar in many respects to that projected by Sir Thomas More, and might have gradually given a turn to men's inclinations and humours, which would have as effectually prevented the establishment of private property, as the violent inclination towards property has hitherto prevented the establishment of a constitution founded on a perfect equality.

Such a supposition includes nothing impossible. Chance must have had a prodigious influence in the first institution of government, and a thousand unknown accidents concurred to turn the attention of mankind either one way, or the contrary. The idea of appropriating particular tracts of the earth, which were originally common to the whole species, though easy and natural to us, may be supposed rather to have appeared unnatural at the beginning. Nothing therefore hinders us to conceive that men might have been originally led to a model of society, without any establishment of property.

But whether it was, or it was not possible at the beginning, to have established such a government, it may be very possible to do it in some future period without any miraculous interposition. In particular, there are two things which, according to the natural course of human affairs, may give occasion to erect such a society.

First, it is possible to establish it even in a civilized country, by means of an extraordinary concurrence of circumstances, at the time of a grand revolution. On such an occasion, a spirit for patriotism and a love of equality may be accidentally raised, and run high. It may chance to be conducted by men of eminence in the state: such as are sprung from noble of from royal blood, like Lycurgus of old, may cheerfully give their assistance, and by their example and authority, engage others in the grand design. Multitudes may be willing to lay down their honors and lucrative employments, and place themselves on a level with the people. The humour may run so fast, and the tide bear so strong, that none shall venture to go against it. A whole nation may be smitten with a generous enthusiasm to sacrifice all private interests to the public good. None of these things are impossible. Enthusiasm has produced as surprising effects on former occasions.

But this is not the only method in which such a constitution may be established. A second is no less possible. A select society of rich Europeans of honest hearts and extensive views, by some particular accidents may become enamoured of such an equal government: they may form a design to give it a beginning, and to try an experiment. Resolving to retire into a country not formerly inhabited, they may persuade their friends and relations to follow them. By considerable rewards, and by the prospect of an easier and more agreeable settlement, they may engage a goodly number of honest and ingenious artists of different kinds to go along with them. They may carry with them great stores of provisions, and all sorts of materials and instruments necessary for their new colony. Concord and wisdom may attend their councils, and Heaven may bless them. Thus they may be able to lay the foundation of an equal government, which being once settled, may happily take such root, and become so powerful, as at first to extend itself to the utmost verge of these uncultivated lands where it was originally settled. Afterwards, by its fair example, it may allure the neighbouring nations to copy after such an excellent model, till at last such governments shall overspread great tracts of the earth, and overcome whatever would oppose them. The advantages of such a constitution may stir up the subjects of the most powerful monarchies to become zealous for such an equitable plan. Their monarchs and great men, may be obliged to give up their prerogatives, and yield to the general desires of the people.

Thus I imagine it possible to establish such a government in some future times, but the probability of doing it is so small, and the prospect is so distant, that modern statesmen will not apprehend any danger to their present systems. In truth, most modern politicians have such confined views, and so little grandeur in their schemes, that they imagine things of much less difficulty to be wholly impracticable. Nay, which is more to be lamented, discard all patriotism, as if it had not any solid foundation in human nature.

It may be observed further, that if the great governor of the world intends to establish such an equitable government, it is perfectly agreeable to the profound wisdom and mysterious workings of his providence, to accomplish this design slowly, imperceptibly, and by intricate operations. He could easily accomplish it at once by miracles, or inspiration; but he does not commonly make choice of supernatural, but of natural methods. There is certainly the most perfect harmony in all the divine councils: the means which God employs, concur in producing the designed effect in the most proper season and manner. Yet there is often an apparent discord in the methods of his procedure. 'Tis often by violent oppositions and discord, that the most perfect concord is at last established.

Thus, if it is the intention of the divine wisdom to carry human society to the greatest perfection of which it is capable on this earth, by means of a perfect government, the design may be laid so deep, and be carried on so slowly, as to require many ages for its accomplishment. 'Tis like art than nature, to form things in their greatest perfection at once. Neither trees, nor corn, nor flowers, grow up to maturity in a day. They increase imperceptibly, and go through various processes. 'Tis only after long periods, that some vegetables arrive at their greatest strength and glory. The more perfect the vegetable, the process is longer and more various. Nature observes a similar analogy in the brute animals. Nor does man arrive at perfection, but by a course of exercise and discipline... Philosophers and law-givers may perhaps arise in different ages and nations, to conceive the idea of perfect governments. Descriptions may be made of them, and be left to posterity. Errors may be detected, and remedies proposed. Different schemes may be explained. A perfect system may happily be found out. Grand revolutions in nations may give it a beginning, and a constitution at length be settled, which is founded on a perfect equality. Such a government, being once established in any particular nation, may, like ancient Rome, but without her enormous ambition, extend its influence to the most distant nations, and cause a total revolution in the notions, dispositions, and affairs of mankind...

But, supposing that governments of such an extraordinary nature, should actually be established by a series of unaccountable accidents; what shall be thought of their duration? Can they have a solid foundation? Or, are the maxims on which they are built, consistent with the natural passions and appetites of mankind? This is the second question: to which many will answer in the negative, though they may possibly admit, that such governments may, or might have been, settled accidentally through some extraordinary concurrence of circumstances, or through a high strain of enthusiasm after some grand revolution. Allowing (will they say) that the great men who had the principal hand in the revolution, had generously yielded up their superiority, and condescended to put themselves on a level with the people; such a high strain of patriotism could not continue long in vigour. The selfish passions of mankind, and their natural love of superiority, though laid asleep at a particular conjuncture, would soon be roused up again, and becoming as restless as ever, would prevail over the weaker efforts of patriotism and a public spirit.

In determining a case so nice and curious, it may seem too bold an assertion that such a government could never degenerate from its primitive purity. All human constitutions seem liable to corruption. Whatever vigour they promised at first, after a certain period they begin to decay. They lose that high spirit with which they were originally actuated. They languish by degrees, till either they are resolved into their first principles, and like animal bodies, renew their strength by some mighty convulsion; or till they are at last dissolved by a violent shock which utterly destroys their frame and constitution.

But, though all constitutions may decay; why may not this form be as durable as any other? There seems to be nothing in the human frame which is inconsistent with the proposed equality, so fundamental in our perfect government; but either,

1. Emulation, envy, a desire of distinction, or, as it may be expressed, the love of preeminence, power, or dominion; all which may be reduced to the same principle, and is called ambition.
2. The love of ease or sensual pleasure.
3. The love of liberty.
4. Interfering passions and appetites, which excite violent struggles by men's fixing their affections on the same objects, which can only be enjoyed by one or by a few.

These are the only principles in human nature which seem contrary to an equal distribution of labour among mankind, and to their equal enjoyment of the advantages which flow from it. I shall examine whether their influence is so pernicious as continually to disturb, and, at last, to be able to overturn the most excellent plan which is founded on equality.

1. Emulation, ambition or the desire of distinction and superiority, must be confessed to be one of our passions. Perhaps it is among the strongest. It is certainly deeply rooted in human nature, and cannot be eradicated. But under an Utopian constitution, there is no necessity that it should; nor indeed, that it should be any weaker than it is at present; since it may be fully gratified, though in a different manner; and since it is not the principle itself, but the object about which it is exercised, that would be varied under such a government.

It is true, many methods by which we distinguish ourselves, and obtain honour under our present models of government, could have no place under a different form, but other distinctions would supply their room, and be in as high a reputation. All those distinctions would remain which are founded on any real virtue or excellency; and those only be wanting which have arisen and grown up from imperfect and confused, or from false and unjust conceptions of worth and dignity, contracted by a bad education under imperfect governments, and preserved by the influence of false discipline and corrupted institutions.

It must be confessed, that in all ages mankind have been passionately fond of the distinctions which arise from elegant and magnificent houses, rich furniture, sumptuous clothing, costly and luxurious tables, numerous attendants, and splendid equipages. Princes have been ambitious to be the masters of large dominions and great armies, and to have an absolute uncontrollable power. Those of an inferior rank, have ardently wished to be favourites at court, or to be idolized by the people. But, it will not follow that under a government where there is no room for such distinctions, mankind would have the same notions of preeminence. Whatever is attended with honour in any country, and under any constitution, will be passionately desired; but where there is no room for distinction, emulation cannot have a place. If we had never heard of a coach and six, or if it had been common to all men, where could there have been a foundation of annexing the idea of superior honour to such a machine? If all men's houses, clothes, and tables are, and must always be equally good; whence could arise the idea of distinction in things of this nature? Our false notions of this kind, flow from our folly under our imperfect governments, in which we may use or abuse our property as we fancy. Hence a weak man becomes proud, and overvalues himself on account of a better house or table. Under our governments, there is an advantage in such superiority. We may display a good understanding and taste, and even a good disposition of heart by such distinctions. But though we suppose the love of preeminence ever so strong among the Utopians, they could never discover it, nor could they be tempted to discover it by finer houses, clothes or tables, which must all be equally good; or by a retinue of servants, when there are none in the country; or by power and influence over a free people altogether unsuitable to their maxims and polity, among whom the employment of a magistrate or overseer, is not more honourable than that of others, and only creates a greater respect in the same manner in which other employments create a respect, by a faithful and diligent discharge and attendance.

Under every government, much depends upon the maxims and customs which have once been established, and have taken a firm root. According to common opinion, many useful and necessary employments amongst us, carry along with them an idea of baseness; nor can men of narrow minds, or such as have never seen or heard of different manners, divest themselves of violent prejudices against them, though there is not any real baseness in such employments.

But under our equal government, all useful trades are honoured. The more laborious they are, "ceteris paribus," they are more highly honoured. Easier and less fatiguing employments, are less respected, unless attended with a proportionably greater diligence. Magistracy, which is nothing but the oversight of others, and under a sound constitution would be among the easiest tasks, would probably procure less regard than what would give less trouble. Even under our imperfect governments, 'tis not so much the labour in itself which excites the idea of meanness, as the circumstances of the persons who are engaged in it. The ignorance of the vulgar, their narrow views, the nastiness of their cottages, their ragged clothes, their scanty tables, and other things of a like nature, are the chief causes which disgrace their employments. Agriculture is in itself the most necessary employment. In certain ages and countries, it has been in high honour. It is not the labour and dirt which attend it, that create the contempt with which it is accompanied at present: else why should not the same contempt be poured on other employments, which not only require toil, but bespatter the clothes and harden the skin. The distinction arises from the characters and circumstances of the persons who are employed in it. In general, labour is so far from drawing down contempt on those who labour, that it procures honour; nay, greater honour in proportion to the greatness of the toil.

If we view things in this light, it will be evident, that where a whole people may be equally wise, where there is not any trade which unfits a man for knowledge, where none are worn out by severe labour, where each person employs only certain hours of the day in some useful business, and may have as fine and elegant a taste, as gentle and polite manners, and spend the rest of his time as agreeably, and with as much ease as any other person, no man's employment can fall into contempt in such circumstances. Do not we see, amidst all our follies and false conceptions, that rich tradesmen of good sense, and agreeable conversation, are much respected, though they have slaved a great deal in their youth, and continue to undergo a great deal of toil on necessary occasions? Do not all wise men prefer them to the richest fool who never spent a day in useful labour, nor ever dirted his clothes in his whole life?

Hence we may be convinced, that the ideas of men who have been born and educated under an equal government, must be very different from the idle conceits which have grown up among us, through the licentiousness of our manners. We may easily see that the Utopians may be very well satisfied with that equality of conditions which is suitable to their own customs, as they cannot have the same ideas of those distinctions which so much disturb mankind under other governments. In truth, all such distinctions would be as unsuitable to their manners, as they are suitable to ours; and the affectation of such distinctions under their form of government, must be no less unnatural, ridiculous, odious and dangerous, than attempts to destroy them under such, governments as ours.

Further; where men do not interfere, and have no opposite interests, envy ceases. No man envies his neighbour the serenity or freshness of the air, plenty of cool water, or any of the comforts of life which we enjoy in common. If our interests do not interfere, we rather rejoice in the general happiness. If all the members of a commonwealth could live in an easy and agreeable way; if they were lodged, clothed, and fed in the same convenient manner, they would have no temptation to seek preeminence by advantages of this kind.

At the same time, we need not suppose them to be without ambition, nor can objects be wanting to satisfy it. The strength and beauty of the body naturally entitle men to regard. Greater sagacity and quickness of the understanding command respect wherever they appear. Men especially, may distinguish themselves under all governments whatsoever, by their virtues, by the superior graces of their character, by their greater diligence in acquiring knowledge and wisdom, by a peculiar activity in their particular employments, by their higher talents in poetry, painting, statuary, oratory, music, architecture, and in all other arts intended either for ornament or use. In truth, it must be as natural under an Utopian government, to seek honour in such righteous and useful pursuits, as to court distinction under other constitutions, by those foolish and destructive practices, which can only be esteemed on account of a general bad taste and depravity of manners. Nay, the subjects of an Utopian government, must be more powerfully excited to distinguish themselves by their superior wisdom and virtue, as they have no other methods of gratifying their ambition.

This is one of the peculiar advantages of such a constitution. It produces wisdom and virtue, as naturally as our imperfect governments produce vice and folly. All its maxims and rules conspire to this excellent purpose.

Thus a government, once happily established upon an equitable footing, may be as durable as any other, notwithstanding the love of distinction, and the powerful principle of ambition so conspicuous in human nature.

2. Such a constitution will not be much in danger from men's love of ease and sensual pleasure, and from their natural aversion to toil and hard labour.

It is, indeed, natural for men to love ease, and to wish that others may rather be obliged to hard labour. Yet it is no less true, that mankind will undergo the greatest toils, submit to the most severe labours, and will encounter the most imminent dangers from a sense of duty, for the sake of honour and glory, or from a prospect of more lasting advantages. Now the Utopians would have the most powerful motives of this kind, to excite them to fulfill their daily tasks with cheerfulness.

The contempt which would follow on idleness, and a refusal to do their duty; the love of their country, and constitution; the plenty which they would enjoy; the examples of industry, that would be every where before their eyes, and that perfect equality which would take place, must be powerful arguments to engage them to diligence. They would sweeten their labours and prevent murmuring; and what is chiefly to be considered, all being employed, and idleness entirely banished, their hardest labours may easily be endured, and are only proper exercises for preserving the health of their bodies, and the vigour of their minds.

Further; in order to prevent strife, there is such an equitable distribution of labour, that when the work is more severe, the time of working is made shorter. Notwithstanding the mildness of their government, there must be a justice and steadiness in the administration, unknown to more imperfect constitutions. Their laws are not without powerful sanctions, to curb the refractory and rebellious. If a spirit of indolence, or pride, should raise up a faction in their country, to exempt themselves from labour, their constitution is better calculated than any other to give check to it, since such a faction having nothing plausible or specious in its pretences, must be extremely odious, and can scarce be supposed to become formidable. In fine, to prevent the possibility of quarreling, and to take away all pretences of murmuring, if any shall scruple to undertake more severe, or more unhealthful labours than what are ordinary, when they are necessary for the state; or shall be unwilling to make a dangerous voyage, or to take up their residence for a time, in a barren, unhealthful, or disagreeable climate, (though on account of the superior honours, which are justly bestowed on whatever can be reckoned heroism, such scruples must be very rare) yet if ever there is any necessity, they determine the case by lot; after which, every one cheerfully submits; it being reckoned one of the most fundamental maxims of their religion and polity to acquiesce in what is considered as the command and determination of providence.

3. After having explained the consistency between an Utopian constitution, and our natural love of honour, ease and pleasure, it will not be necessary to bring a long proof, that the love of liberty is not dangerous to our equal government.

Liberty is more or less restrained under every government. Nor ought it any where to be less restrained, than is necessary for the public good. There may be too much as well as too little liberty; and under all other governments, except the Utopian, there is either too little or too much.

In the greatest part of the world, so little regard has been showed to liberty, that mankind have been subjected to absolute monarchs from generation to generation. This fatal and absurd policy, has too much prevailed in all ages. Scarce was any other government ever known in the East; and great efforts have been made by princes and their ministers, to reduce Europe to the same slavish subjection. However, slavery could never be firmly established in the West. It was chiefly under the Roman Empire, that Liberty was subdued in Europe. It had flourished greatly in the more ancient ages. The nations which destroyed the Roman Empire, however barbarous in other respects, were favourers of free governments. Though they had kings with some high prerogatives, yet certain powers were also invested in the nobles, and in other orders of the state, by which the authority of their kings was limited. Thus, jurisdictions were balanced, and liberty was in some measure secured, 'till the ambition of princes gradually breaking through these limitations, too successful attempts have been made in modern times to reestablish despotism. Nay, within the three last centuries, slavery has even been reduced to a system. This slavish system has been openly avowed. Instead of being ashamed of slavery, an abject spirit of submitting to tyranny, and holding the authority of tyrants sacred, has been reputed honourable. Hence the many strenuous defenders of the absolute power of princes, of the indefeasible right of their heirs to succeed to their despotic power, and of the unlawfulness of resisting them in any case, or upon any pretence whatsoever. This is the system, which, under the notion of supporting loyalty, asserting the rights of Princes, preserving peace, preventing faction, and rendering society more stable, some noted philosophers have maintained to be agreeable to nature, historians to be confirmed by experience, lawyers to be established in law, and divines to be founded on the gospel. Nay, these last gentlemen have enforced it upon our consciences, under the pain of eternal damnation. A few nations excepted, this monstrous system is at this very moment received in all the kingdoms of this earth, and has spread its baleful influence far and near. Such has been the wretched condition of the greatest part of the world.

In governments of this kind, the monarch seldom indulges his subjects in any liberty, but what promotes some real or imaginary advantage to himself and his favourites. In other cases, he allows his people to be as wicked and wretched as they please. What else can be expected? Such tyrants, and their ministers can scarce be supposed to have any idea of a public, and of modeling governments for the public benefit.

But even in those few countries where this doctrine has been exploded, and where law-givers have taken care to provide against absolute and arbitrary power in the hands of a monarch, by dividing authority among different persons and bodies politic; scarce have they aimed at any thing further than to secure the people against oppression by the governors, and to punish a few heinous crimes. Even under free governments, due attention has not been given to the education of the youth; nor has such an excellent discipline, and such wise forms of living, been established, as might have prevented crimes, and trained up the subjects to wisdom and virtue.

Such an excellent polity has indeed been greatly neglected in all ages. Sufficient care has never been taken to form manners, to introduce right fashions, to curb appetite, to guard against a baneful subjection, to the irregularity of passion, and to excite generous and noble sentiments. Fashion and law, have pointed different ways. One practice has been reputed legal, and the contrary honourable. Yet all ages have not been equally faulty. Ancient law-givers had nobler aims than modern statesmen, and showed a greater desire to secure the virtue of the people. They attempted at least, to regulate manners. They made it evident, that they comprehended this under the idea of government. They endeavoured, however unsuccessfully, to train up men to virtue. But the moderns, though they profess to lay down rules for education, and would not be thought to neglect what is so important, have not had such just views of this matter as the ancients. They have scarce considered education as belonging to the public. They have left the instruction of youth, and the distribution of trades and employments, to parents, or to every one's own fancy. Too great regard is shown to the rank, or the riches of the parent. Too much indulgence is given to inclination and humour. The people in general are not laid under such proper and wholesome restraints, as are equally profitable to themselves, and are necessary to make them co-operate towards the general good. The ancients did too little in this way, but the moderns much less; and now, under the very best governments, rich men are allowed to spend their time and their money, to do something or nothing, to marry, or to abstain from marriage, and to educate their children as they please. About all these things, though of the greatest importance, even free governments seem to be too little anxious; leaving the people to be idle, lewd, and voluptuous; to contract all kinds of bad habits, to gratify all their whims and fancies, though infinitely pernicious both to themselves and the public; provided only they do not invade property, nor give any disturbance to others, in indulging in the same boasted but dangerous liberty.

Under the Utopian government, such destructive liberty is not allowed, but licentiousness is curbed with the strictest care. However, real liberty, or the liberty of indulging ourselves freely in every thing agreeable to nature and reason, no where flourishes with such security. Where such an equality is preserved, scarce can we suppose liberty to be in danger. Nor can the highest love of liberty ever be supposed dangerous, under such an equitable constitution.

4. Neither will it be difficult to show that our Utopian government may be firm and permanent, notwithstanding those quarrels which arise from men's affections, chancing to fix upon objects which a few or one only can enjoy. Such quarrels must certainly happen among other accidents. In love no rival can be endured. Hence, those fatal quarrels to which death alone puts an end. Nor is it possible, in many other cases, to prevent all rivalry in human society. But other rivalries can scarce be supposed to bring about great revolutions, if the danger from rivalries in ambi-

tion can be prevented. Inferior rivalries will have an influence on the fate of particular persons; but as few are interested in them, they will have little influence on the public; and a state secure against rivalries of an higher nature, will be safe from convulsions on account of less interesting quarrels.

Upon the whole, if such a constitution is once firmly established, it will suffer as little from the reigning passions of mankind as any other government, and may be fully as durable. 'Tis too bold to assert, that any human constitution can be exempted from all possibility of change. The best constitutions may deviate from their original principles, and gradually lose their primitive vigour; corruption is too natural to mankind, and to all their schemes in this present state, to be infallibly excluded. If our first parents fell from their pure original, who can be secure of their posterity? No government can render mankind absolutely perfect. If any one could, such a one as that of Sir Thomas More's Utopia has the fairest claim. Such a government, so far from being inconsistent with the human frame, or incapable of duration, is bitter balanced and contains fewer seeds of corruption than any other. If it were once firmly established, it may justly be presumed, that it would produce such eminent examples, and would render mankind so wise, so good, and so happy, as would excite a wonderful love of its forms and institutions.

There are two things especially which disturb government, from both of which such a commonwealth would be better secured than any other.

I. The great inequality among mankind, and the advantages enjoyed by a few, which they neither deserve, nor employ for good purposes.

II. The want of a proper education and discipline of the youth.

1. In all our constitutions, there are many offices which are both honourable and lucrative. Such offices are not always conferred on persons of capacity, and probity, who make a proper use of their authority and superior advantages for the public good. They are often bestowed wantonly on men of little merit, or little capacity; while the most useful and laborious part of mankind, are treated with contempt, are suffered to live and die in poverty, and have poverty entailed upon their posterity. How often do the most worthless enjoy great honours and estates from

their ancestors, or by the foolish and indiscreet favour of princes, by the influence of friends, and by the wicked arts of party and cabal? Seldom can one absolutely expect promotion on account of his capacity or merit; after his most strenuous efforts, a faction frequently throws him at a distance, and a worthless rival is preferred. Tyranny is mingled with all our governments: it is either interwoven in the very frame of the constitution, or arises from errors in the administration, or from the superior influence of the great. By means of this tyranny, the lowest and weakest of the people are often oppressed; while those of higher rank, and of greater spirit and capacity are provoked. Hence such frequent murmurs, such dangerous convulsions, such fatal revolutions. What else can be expected? Can it be expected that men of sense and spirit, should not be provoked by observing weak, insolent, and profligate men enjoying those advantages to which they justly conceive they have a better title? How natural is the attempt to make this title good, by improving the opportunities which arise from the blunders and tyranny of their rivals in power? Hence our governments are changeable and unsteady. Hence many factions and cabals for power and dominion in the very best of governments, and under the very best of administrations.

For it must be observed, that these vices and defects of which mankind have been complaining in all ages, are not to be imputed to any one particular kind of government, or administration, exclusive of all others, but are to be found in a less or greater degree in all governments, and under all administrations, the Utopian excepted; they arise from the intrinsic nature of the governments themselves, in which there must happen thousands of accidents, errors, and hardships, which cannot possibly be prevented by the governors, though there may be many among them of the highest abilities, as well as of the most upright intentions and greatest integrity.

But under such a government as we have described, the equitable distribution of labour, and of the profits of it, would take away the occasion of hardships and dangerous cabals. As by removing property, we destroy theft and robbery; so by maintaining an equality, we prevent hardships, banish discord, and restore the golden age. Under such a constitution, men would live in peace and friendship, they would mutually assist one another, by their united labours they would cultivate the earth, and advance continually in knowledge; nor would there be any place for an enormous ambition, which wastes kingdoms, and causes such havoc and desolation in the earth... How could pride and ambition grow up to a dangerous height, with such an education as would be natural in such a government, or with such examples as would be the natural consequence of such an education? It is the want of a proper discipline and education of the youth, which is the second great source of our vices and wretchedness, and which renders our governments so changeable and unsteady.

2. Mankind being vicious and corrupted, have not an idea of that high virtue of which their nature is capable. Depraved themselves, they are negligent in educating their children. Good men are often indolent, or too much employed otherwise. Many are ignorant, and have not a sufficient capacity; or they are poor, and have not the means for giving their children a proper education. Even when the parents are careful and able, their endeavours are often disappointed by the poisonous examples of other children who are ill educated. In short, the world being once corrupted, this corruption cannot be rooted out. Ignorance and wicked maxims prevail, and a wrong taste is propagated from age to age.

Corruption, is indeed natural to mankind. Forwardness, and a lust of power, appear early in children. The seeds of pride and tyranny seem to be deeply rooted in their constitution. Yet, were they not cherished by the wretched taste of parents and nurses, were they properly curbed by an early discipline, they would seldom grow up to monstrous heights. With proper management, good dispositions might be so effectually instilled into youth, as would prevent such a deluge of vice as has overwhelmed the world. Some particular dispositions might perhaps be incurable. Yet there would be few of so perverse a nature, and these few would meet with so many discouragements and checks, as would prevent any dangerous alterations in the state. Thus this happy government would be the firmest of any; and nothing would give reason to apprehend a change, but the uncertainty of all human affairs, and the continual vicissitudes to which mankind are exposed in this imperfect state.

How happy would be the consequences of such an excellent government! Every discouragement to marriage would be effectually removed. Wise regulations would be established to gratify the natural passion of love, in an easy and agreeable manner. No false maxims which corrupt the taste in this grand concern would be in vogue; nor any temptation from interest to mislead the choice. Poverty being effectually banished, and every one upon an equal footing, the numerous impediments arising from an inequality of rank, estates, or other circumstances, would be wholly removed. In this situation, according to the original blessing and command, mankind would be fruitful, and multiply, replenish the earth, and subdue it. By the help of such vast numbers living without anxiety, and in a goodly correspondence, they would be able to cultivate every spot that was habitable in the manner most suitable to its nature. By their united labours, they would raise the most magnificent works, and add innumerable beauties to the face of the earth. Knowledge would increase wonderfully by experiments made at leisure, and with exactness, in all places of the earth; which would be freely communicated every where, and be regularly transmitted to posterity. An unconceivable progress would be made in discovering the laws of nature. There would be proportionable advances in all sorts of useful, ingenious, and agreeable arts. Every one might have the means of being a philosopher if he pleased. A happy emulation, or love of glory; an insatiable curiosity; the love of truth, and an ardent thirst after knowledge, would render men more ingenious, and more successful in making useful discoveries, than either their present wants and necessities, or their love of gain. Scarce can any thing be supposed so difficult to be discovered or effected, that it would not yield to the united efforts of mankind in such a favourable situation. In short, the whole earth would become a paradise, and mankind be universally wise and happy.

PROSPECT IV.

The preceding Model of Government, though consistent with the Human Passions and Appetites, is upon the whole inconsistent with the Circumstances of Mankind upon the Earth.

By this time, I dare say my reader has pronounced me to be an enthusiastic admirer of the Utopian schemes, and an enemy to all inequality of rank, wealth and fortune among men: nor is the charge, perhaps, altogether without foundation. The establishment of property in lands, has been attended with many disadvantages; it seems indeed to have been one great source, not only of those calamities, but of those vices, which have been so sensibly felt, and so loudly complained of in every age. At the same time, so far is it from appearing to have been necessary at the first constitution of society, that it seems rather to have been owing to accidents that it was first thought of, or that mankind consented to make such an experiment. Being ignorant and destitute of experience in what is called the state of nature, feeling the evils of their defenseless and indigent condition; having abundance of room in these early days, and not foreseeing the evils to which the establishment of property would give occasion, they unfortunately had their first recourse to this expedient, instead of agreeing to an equitable distribution of labour, and to a community of goods. But if we consider their circumstances at that time, before any particular spots of the earth had been appropriated by individuals, the establishment of property does not appear to be the most natural and obvious scheme of promoting peace and union. Instead of dividing the lands among particular persons, might they not have consented to labour them in common, and share equally of the fruits? They would have found this rather more easy; and if they had fallen into this tract at the beginning, and made some essays of this kind, though rude and imperfect, they might have been taught by experience to correct their errors, and possibly might at last have set their affairs upon a better footing than ever they have been hitherto.

...

But... it deserves our particular attention, That as no government which has hitherto been established, is free from all seeds of corruption, or can be expected to be eternal; so if we suppose a government to be perfect in its original frame, and to be administered in the most perfect manner, after whatever model we suppose it to have been framed, such a perfect form would be so far from lasting for ever, that it must come to an end so much the sooner on account of its perfection. For, though happily such governments should be firmly established, though they should be found consistent with the reigning passions of human nature, though they should spread far and wide; nay, though they should prevail universally, they must at last involve mankind in the deepest perplexity, and in universal confusion. For however excellent they may be in their own nature, they are altogether inconsistent with the present frame of nature, and with a limited extent of earth.

Under a perfect government, the inconveniences of having a family would be so entirely removed, children would be so well taken care of, and every thing become so favourable to populousness, that though some sickly seasons or dreadful plagues in particular climates might cut off multitudes, yet in general, mankind would increase so prodigiously, that the earth would at last be overstocked, and become unable to support its numerous inhabitants.

How long the earth, with the best culture of which it is capable from human genius and industry, might be able to nourish its perpetually increasing inhabitants, is as impossible as it is unnecessary to be determined. It is not probable that it could have supported them during so long a period as since the creation of Adam. But whatever may be supposed of the length of this period, of necessity it must be granted, that the earth could not nourish them for ever, unless either its fertility could be continually augmented, or by some secret in nature, like what certain enthusiasts have expected from the philosophers stone, some wise adept in the occult sciences, should invent a method of supporting mankind quite different from any thing known at present. Nay, though some extraordinary method of supporting them might possibly be found out, yet if there was no bound to the increase of mankind, which would be the case under a perfect government, there would not even be sufficient room for containing their bodies upon the surface of the earth, or upon any limited surface whatsoever. It would be necessary, therefore, in order to find room for such multitudes of men, that the earth should be continually enlarging in bulk, as an animal or vegetable body.

Now since philosophers may as soon attempt to make mankind immortal, as to support the animal frame without food; it is equally certain, that limits are set to the fertility of the earth, and that its bulk, so far as is hitherto known, has continued always the same, and probably could not be much altered without making considerable changes in the solar system. It would be impossible, therefore, to support the great numbers of men who would be raised up under a perfect government; the earth would be overstocked at last, and the greatest admirers of such fanciful schemes must foresee the fatal period when they would come to an end, as they are altogether inconsistent with the limits of that earth in which they must exist.

What a miserable catastrophe of the most generous of all human systems of government! How dreadfully would the magistrates of such commonwealths find themselves disconcerted at that fatal period, when there was no longer any room for new colonies, and when the earth could produce no further supplies! During all the preceding ages, while there was room for increase, mankind must have been happy; the earth must have been a paradise in the literal sense, as the greatest part of it must have been turned into delightful and fruitful gardens. But when the dreadful time should at last come, when our globe, by the most diligent culture, could not produce what was sufficient to nourish its numerous inhabitants, what happy expedient could then be found out to remedy so great an evil?

In such a cruel necessity, must there be a law to restrain marriage? Must multitudes of women, be shut up in cloisters like the ancient vestals or modern nuns? To keep a balance between the two sexes, must a proportionate number of men be debarred from marriage? Shall the Utopians, following the wicked policy of superstition, forbid their priests to marry; or shall they rather sacrifice men of some other profession for the good of the state? Or, shall they appoint the sons of certain families to be maimed at their birth, and give a sanction to the unnatural institution of eunuchs? If none of these expedients can be thought proper, shall they appoint a certain number of infants to be exposed to death as soon as they are born, determining the proportion according to the exigencies of the state; and pointing out the particular victims by lot, or according to some established rule? Or, must they shorten the period of human life by a law, and condemn all to die after they had completed a certain age, which might be shorter or longer, as provisions were either more scanty or plentiful? Or what other method should they devise (for an expedient would be absolutely necessary) to restrain the number of citizens within reasonable bounds?

Alas! How unnatural and inhuman must every such expedient be accounted! The natural passions and appetites of mankind are planted in our frame, to answer the best ends for the happiness both of the individuals and of the species. Shall we be obliged to contradict such a wise order? Shall we be laid under the necessity of acting barbarously and inhumanly? Sad and fatal necessity! And which, after all, could never answer the end, but would give rise to violence and war. For mankind would never agree about such regulations. Force, and arms, must at last decide their quarrels, and the deaths of such as fall in battle, leave sufficient provisions for the survivors, and make room for others to be born.

Thus the tranquility and numerous blessings of the Utopian governments would come to an end; war, or cruel and unnatural customs, be introduced, and a stop put to the increase of mankind, to the advancement of knowledge; and to the culture of the earth, in spite of the most excellent laws and wisest precautions. The more excellent the laws had been, and the more strictly they had been observed, mankind must have sooner become miserable. The remembrance of former times, the greatness of their wisdom and virtue, would conspire to heighten their distress; and the world, instead of remaining the mansion of wisdom and happiness, become the scene of vice and confusion. Force and fraud must prevail, and mankind be reduced to the same calamitous condition as at present.

...

By reasoning in this manner, it is not pretended that 'tis unnatural to set bounds to human knowledge and happiness, or to the grandeur of society, and to confine what is finite to proper limits. It is certainly fit to set just bounds to every thing according to its nature, and to adjust all things in due proportion to one another. Undoubtedly, such an excellent order is actually established throughout all the works of God in his wide dominions. But there are certain primary determinations in nature, to which all other things of a subordinate kind must be adjusted. A limited earth, a limited degree of fertility, and the continual increase of mankind are three of these original constitutions. To these determinations, human affairs, and the circumstances of all other animals, must be adapted. In which view, it is unsuitable to our ideas of order, that while the earth is only capable of maintaining a determined number, the human race should increase without end. This would be the necessary consequence of a perfect government and education. On which account it is more contrary to just proportion, to suppose that such a perfect government should be established in such circumstances, than that by permitting vice, or the abuse of liberty in the wisdom of providence, mankind should never be able to multiply so greatly as to overstock the earth.

From this view of the circumstances of the world, notwithstanding the high opinion we have of the merit of Sir Thomas More, and other admired projectors of perfect governments in ancient or modern times, we may discern how little can be expected from their most perfect systems.

As for these worthy philosophers, patriots, and law-givers, who have employed their time and their talents in framing such excellent models, we ought to do justice to their characters, and gratefully to acknowledge their generous efforts to rescue the world out of that distress into which it has fallen, through the imperfection of government. Sincere, and ardent in their love of virtue, enamoured of its lovely form, deeply interested for the happiness of mankind to the best of their skill, and with hearts full of zeal, they have strenuously endeavoured to advance human society to perfection. For this, their memory ought to be sacred to posterity. But if they expected their beautiful systems actually to take place, their hopes were ill founded, and they were not sufficiently aware of the consequences.

The speculations of such ingenious authors enlarge our views, and amuse our fancies. They are useful for directing us to correct certain errors at particular times. Able legislators ought to consider them as models, and honest patriots ought never to lose sight of them, or any proper opportunity of transplanting the wisest of their maxims into their own governments, as far as they are adapted to their particular circumstances, and will give no occasion to dangerous convulsions. But this is all that can be expected. Though such ingenious romances should chance to be read and admired, jealous and selfish politicians need not be alarmed. Such statesmen need not fear that ever such airy systems shall be able to destroy their craft, or disappoint them of their intention to sacrifice the interest of mankind to their own avarice or ambition. There is too powerful a charm which works secretly in favour of such politicians, which will for ever defeat all attempts to establish a perfect government. There is no need of miracles for this purpose. The vices of mankind are sufficient. And we need not doubt but providence will make use of them, for preventing the establishment of governments which are by no means suitable to the present circumstances of the earth.

Six
William Ogilvie
(1736–1819)

AN ESSAY ON THE RIGHT OF PROPERTY IN LAND
(1782)

INTRODUCTION

The municipal laws of every country are not only observed as a rule of conduct, but by the bulk of the people they are regarded as the standard of right and of wrong, in all matters to which their regulations are extended.

In this prejudice, however natural to the crowd, and however salutary it may be deemed, men of enlarged and inquisitive minds are bound by no ties to acquiesce without inquiry.

Property is one of the principal objects of municipal law, and that to which its regulations are applied with greatest efficacy and precision. With respect to property in movables, great uniformity takes place in the laws of almost all nations; they differ only as being more or less extended to details, comprehending the diversity of commercial transactions; and this branch of jurisprudence may be said to have almost attained to its ultimate maturity and perfection.

But with respect to property in land, different principles have been adopted by different nations in different ages; and there is no reason why that system, which now prevails in Europe, and which is derived from an age, not deserving to be extolled for legislative wisdom, or regard to the equal rights of men, should be supposed to excel any system that has taken place elsewhere, or to be in itself already advanced beyond the capacity of improvement, or the need of reformation.

It is to a free and speculative disquisition, concerning the foundation of this right of property in land, and concerning those modifications, by which it may be rendered in the highest degree beneficial to all ranks of men, that the author of these pages wishes to call the attention of the learned, the ingenious, and the friends of mankind.

It can give him no surprise, if the opinions he has advanced on a topic of discussion, so new, and so interesting to all, shall meet with the approbation of a few only. Were they now for the first time to be presented abruptly to his own mind, he believes that they would startle his first thoughts, and perhaps might be rejected on a transient view. But the leading principles of that system, which he now holds, respecting property in land, have been coeval in his mind with the free exercise of his thoughts in speculative inquiries; they have recurred often, they have been gradually unfolded, and for some years past he has been accustomed to review them frequently, almost in their present form, with still increasing approbation.

All that he would request in their favour (and the candid will readily grant this) is, that they may not be rejected on a first disgust, and that those who cannot adopt the opinions here advanced may at least bestow some pains in ascertaining their own. These are the opinions of one individual, thinking freely, and for himself; they are erroneous perhaps and visionary; their singularity may well authorize a suspicion that they are so, and this suspicion ought to have kept them back from the public eye, but for the hope of exciting others to enter into the same train of inquiry, and no longer, in a matter of the first importance to the interests of society, implicitly to acquiesce in traditional doctrines, never yet submitted to examination.

Free inquiry, however it may give birth to vain theories and chimerical projects, has never in any department been productive of essential detriment to the true interests of mankind. What undesirable consequences have always arisen from the stagnation of inquiry, and from silent acquiescence, even in establishments that are beneficial, and in opinions that are true, the history of mankind bears witness in every age.

It is natural to the mind, when new ideas arise on important subjects, to open itself with fondness to the pleasing impression which they make. Yielding to this seducing enthusiasm, the author has been led to speak with freedom of great changes, suddenly to be accomplished, as practicable in some cases, and to be desired in many. Yet is he well aware that great changes, suddenly accomplished, are always pregnant with danger, and with evil, and ought on almost no occasion whatever to be desired, or brought forward by the friends of mankind. Partial reformation, gradual progressive innovation, may produce every advantage which the most important and sudden changes can promise, yet without incurring those dreadful hazards, and those inevitable evils, with which great and sudden changes are still attended.

With the greatest satisfaction of mind he avows his persuasion, that were great and important innovations respecting property in land as practicable and safe, as they are difficult and full of danger, there is no country under the sun which stands less in need of such reformation than England. Although indeed the principles of jurisprudence, respecting property in land, which the laws of England recognize, are derived from the same source, and partake of the same absurd and pernicious nature with those maxims which prevail almost everywhere on the continent of Europe, yet such has been the generosity of English landholders, such their equitable conduct towards their tenants and dependants, and such the manly spirit of the lower classes, fostered by a sense of political rights, that in England the comfortable independence of the farmer and actual cultivator of the soil, is established on as secure a footing as the most refined system of property in land deduced from the genuine principles of public good and natural right can propose to render effectual and permanent. It is to be regretted only that this comfortable independence which the farmers enjoy cannot be extended to a still greater proportion of the community. English landholders and English farmers are superior in all respects to the same class of men in other countries: in their manly vigour, their plain good sense, their humane virtues, consists the true basis of our national preeminence. Their blood circulates in every rank of society, their domestic manners have given the tone to the English character as displayed in all the various departments of business and enterprise; nor can any wish be formed more favourable to the prosperity of the public, than that the numbers of this class of men may be increased. To increase the number of landholders by advancing farmers to that more independent situation, can never be made the object of legislative care in this country, as it might in the absolute monarchies of the continent; but to increase the number of farmers, by favouring the advancement of day labourers and manufacturers to the more animating and manly occupation of cultivating a small farm for their own account, is an object very similar to many branches of enlightened policy which the British legislature (more than any other) has pursued with attention and success.

To the worthy and humane English landholders, and more particularly to those who of late years have voluntarily granted to their tenants an abatement of rent, this short Essay is inscribed by the Author, as to men whom he regards with high esteem, and from whom he may hope that his speculations, should they ever come to their knowledge, would meet with no unfavourable reception. Why should he not flatter himself with this hope, however seemingly vain, since uninformed by theoretical reasonings, and prompted only by the innate candour and humanity of their own minds, these respectable landholders, truly worthy of their station and of their trust, have habitually acted in conformity to those principles of public good and natural right which he is desirous to elucidate and establish.

PART I.

SECTION I. *Of the Right of Property in Land as derived from the Law of Nature.*

1. All right of property is founded either in occupancy or labour. The earth having been given to mankind in common occupancy, each individual seems to have by nature a right to possess and cultivate an equal share. This right is little different from that which he has to the free use of the open air and running water; though not so indispensably requisite at short intervals for his actual existence, it is not less essential to the welfare and right state of his life through all its progressive stages.

2. No individual can derive from this general right of occupancy a title to any more than an equal share of the soil of his country. His actual possession of more cannot of right preclude the claim of any other person who is not already possessed of such equal share.

3. This title to an equal share of property in land seems original, inherent, and indefeasible by any act or determination of others, though capable of being alienated by our own. It is a birthright

which every citizen still retains. Though by entering into society and partaking of its advantages, he must be supposed to have submitted this natural right to such regulations as may be established for the general good, yet he can never be understood to have tacitly renounced it altogether; nor ought anything less to establish such alienation than an express compact in mature age, after having been in actual possession, or having had a free opportunity of entering into the possession of his equal share.

4. Every state or community ought in justice to reserve for all its citizens the opportunities of entering upon, or returning to, and resuming this their birthright and natural employment, whenever they are inclined to do so.

Whatever inconveniences may be thought to accompany this reservation, they ought not to stand in the way of essential justice.

Although at first sight such reservation may appear incompatible with the established order of societies and the permanent cultivation of the earth, yet ought it on the other hand to be presumed, that what is so plainly founded on the natural rights of men, may by wise regulations be rendered at least consistent with the best order and prosperity of societies, and with the progress of agriculture; perhaps, very beneficial to the one, and the highest encouragement to the other.

5. In many rude communities, this original right has been respected, and their public institutions accommodated to it, by annual, or at least frequent partitions of the soil, as among the ancient Germans, and among the native Irish even in Spenser's time.

Wherever conquests have taken place, this right has been commonly subverted and effaced. In the progress of commercial arts and refinements, it is suffered to fall into obscurity and neglect.

6. Whatever has been advanced by Mr. Locke and his followers, concerning the right of property in land, as independent of the laws of a higher original than they, and of a nature almost similar to that divine right of kings, which their antagonists had maintained, can only be referred to this original right of equal property in land, founded on that general right of occupancy, which the whole community has, to the territory of the State. This equal right is indeed antecedent to municipal laws, and not to be abolished by them. But it were a mistake to ascribe any such sacred and indefeasible nature to that sort of property in land which is established by the regulations of municipal law, which

has its foundation in the right of labour, and may be acquired by individuals, in very unequal degrees of extent, and to the accumulation of which very few states have thought fit to set any limits.

7. That right which the landholder has to an estate, consisting of a thousand times his own original equal share of the soil, cannot be founded in the general right of occupancy, but in the labour which he and those to whom he has succeeded, or from whom he has purchased, have bestowed on the improvement and fertilization of the soil. To this extent, it is natural and just: but such a right founded in labour cannot supersede that natural right of occupancy, which nine hundred and ninety-nine other persons have to their equal shares of the soil, in its original state. Although it may bar the claim of individuals, it cannot preclude that of the legislature, as trustee and guardian of the whole.

8. In every country where agriculture has made considerable progress, these two rights are blended together, and that which has its origin in labour is suffered to eclipse the other, founded in occupancy. As the whole extent of soil is affected by both rights at once, and not different parts by each; as these rights subsist together in the same subject, the limits by which their influence and extent may be discriminated from each other do not readily present themselves to the mind; and could these limits be distinctly ascertained, it may seem still more difficult to suggest any practicable method by which the subjects of each could be actually separated and detached.

9. That every man has a right to an equal share of the soil, in its original state, may be admitted to be a maxim of natural law. It is also a maxim of natural law, that every one, by whose labour any portion of the soil has been rendered more fertile, has a right to the additional produce of that fertility, or to the value of it, and may transmit this right to other men. On the first of these maxims depend the freedom and prosperity of the lower ranks. On the second, the perfection of the art of agriculture, and the improvement of the common stock and wealth of the community. Did the laws of any country pay equal regard to both these maxims, so as they might be made to produce their respective good effects, without entrenching on one another, the highest degree of public prosperity would result from this combination.

10. Plans for the establishment of this combination are not, it must be owned, very obvious, nor have they on the other hand

been very industriously sought for. Scarcely has any nation actually carried or attempted to carry into execution any plan having this for its object; and not many can be said to have attained in any period of their history those enlarged views of the public interest which might lead to the investigation or establishment of such a plan.

Rude nations have adhered to the first of these maxims, neglecting the second. Nations advanced in industry and arts have adhered to the second, neglecting the first.

Could any plan be proposed for uniting these two maxims in operation and effect, still, in rich and industrious nations, the supposed (not the real) interests of the less numerous but more powerful orders of men, would be found in opposition to its establishment.

11. To establish a just combination of these two maxims, at the original foundation of states, so as to render it a fundamental part of their frame and constitution, or to introduce it afterwards with as little violence as may be, to the actual possessions and supposed rights and interests of various orders of men, ought to be the object of all Agrarian laws; and this object being once distinctly conceived, if wise and benevolent men will turn their attention towards it, no doubt need be entertained that very practicable methods of carrying it into execution will in time be discovered, by comparison of projects, or from the result of trials.

12. When any piece of land is sold, the price paid by the purchaser may be considered as consisting of three parts, each being the value of a distinct subject, the separate amount of which, men skilful in agriculture, and acquainted with the soil of the country, might accurately enough appreciate.

These parts are:

(1st.) The *original* value of the soil, or that which it might have borne in its natural state, prior to all cultivation.

(2nd.) The *accessory* or *improved* value of the soil: that, to wit, which it has received from the improvements and cultivation bestowed on it by the last proprietor, and those who have preceded him.

(3rd.) The *contingent*, or *improvable* value of the soil: that further value which it may still receive from future cultivation and improvements, over and above defraying the expense of making such improvements; or, as it may be otherwise expressed, the value of an exclusive right to make these improvements.

If, in England, 100 acres of arable are sold for £1500, money being at 5 per cent, the contingent value may be reckoned £500 for the superior value of that security which land gives may, in a general argument, be supposed to be counterbalanced by the trouble of management. Of the remaining £1000, two or three hundred may be computed to be the original value of the soil, a judgment being formed from the nature of the adjoining common, and the £700 or £800 remaining is to be accounted the amount of the accessory or improved value. In this example, these three parts of the general value are to one another as 2, 8, and 5. If the example is taken from a hundred acres in Bengal, or the lower Egypt, the proportion of the parts may be supposed to be 10, 4, and 1. If from 100 acres of uncultivated moorland, in Ireland, or the northern counties of England, the proportion of the parts may be as 1, 0, and 14.

13. The estate of every landholder may, while he possesses it, be considered as capable of being analysed into these three component parts; and could the value of each be separately ascertained by any equitable method (as by the verdict of an assize), it would not be difficult to distinguish the nature and the extent of his private right, and of that right also which still belongs to the community, in those fields which he is permitted, under the protection of municipal law, to possess. He must be allowed to have a full and absolute right to the original, the improved, and contingent value of such portion of his estate, as would fall to his share, on an equal partition of the territory of the State among the citizens. Over all the surplus extent of his estate, he has a full right to the whole accessory value, whether he has been the original improver himself, or has succeeded to, or purchased from the heirs or assignees of such improver. But to the original and contingent value of this surplus extent he has no full right. That must still reside in the community at large, and, though seemingly neglected or relinquished, may be claimed at pleasure by the legislature, or by the magistrate, who is the public trustee.

14. The difficulty of ascertaining these different sorts of value, and of separating them from one another, if ascertained, may be supposed in general to have prevented such claims from being made. It is particularly difficult to distinguish the original from the accessory value; nor is the community much injured by suffering these to remain together in the hands of the greater landholders, especially in countries where land-taxes make a principal branch of the public revenue, and no tax is imposed on property

of other kinds. The original value of the soil is, in such states, in fact, treated as a fund belonging to the public, and merely deposited in the hands of great proprietors, to be, by the imposition of land-taxes, gradually applied to the public use, and which may be justly drawn from them, as the public occasions require, until the whole be exhausted. Equity, however, requires that from such land-taxes those small tenements which do not exceed the proprietor's natural share of the soil should be exempted. To separate the contingent value from the other two is less difficult, and of more importance; for the detriment which the public suffers by neglecting this separation, and permitting an exclusive right of improving the soil to accumulate in the hands of a small part of the community, is far greater, in respect both of the progress of agriculture, and the comfortable independence of the lower ranks.

SECTION II. *Of the Right of Property in Land, as founded on public Utility.*

15. The increase of public happiness is the true primary object which ought to claim the attention of every state. It is to be attained by increasing the common standard or measure of happiness, which every citizen may have a chance of enjoying under the protection of the State; and by increasing the number of citizens, who are to enjoy this common measure of happiness. The increase of opulence, or of dominion, are subordinate objects, and only to be pursued, as they tend to the increase of happiness, or of numbers; to both of which they are in some respects, and in certain cases, unfriendly.

16. Whatever regulations tend directly to increase the common measure of happiness, enjoyed by each individual citizen, tend assuredly to increase the number of citizens. But every regulation tending to increase the number of citizens does not certainly tend to increase the common measure of happiness, and in various situations of the community, may tend to diminish it. The first sort of regulations is therefore to be preferred, in case of interference, to the second.

17. The happiness of individuals, or of any great body of men, is nearly in proportion to their virtue and their worth. That manner of life, therefore, which is most favourable to the virtue of the citizens, ought, for the sake of their happiness, to be encouraged

and promoted by the legislature. Men employed in cultivating the soil, if suffered to enjoy a reasonable independence, and a just share of the produce of their toil, are of simpler manners, and more virtuous, honest dispositions, than any other class of men. The testimony of all observers, in every age and country, concurs in this, and the reason of it may be found in the nature of their industry, and its reward. Their industry is not like that of the labouring manufacturer, insipidly uniform, but varied, it excludes idleness without imposing excessive drudgery, and its reward consists in abundance of necessary accommodations, without luxury and refinement.

18. The families which are employed in this healthful industry, and live in this comfortable independence, increase more than others in different situations of life. It is by their progeny chiefly that the waste of great cities, of armies, navies, commercial and manufacturing occupations is continually supplied.

19. The labour of men applied to the cultivation of the earth tends more to increase the public wealth, for it is more productive of things necessary for the accommodation of life, wherein all real wealth consists, than if it were applied to any other purpose; and all labour applied to refined and commercial arts, while the State can furnish or procure opportunities of applying it to the cultivation of the soil, may be said to be squandered and misapplied, unless in so far as it is given to those liberal arts, whose productions operate on the mind, and rouse the fancy or the heart.

20. The most obvious, the surest, and least equivocal indication of prosperity and happiness is the strength and comeliness of a race of men.

21. Those who are employed in agriculture, if not oppressed by the superior orders, if permitted to enjoy competent independence and rustic plenty, remote from the contagion of intemperance, are known to excel in strength, comeliness, and good health, every other class of men in civilized nations; and are only excelled in those respects by some simple tribes of men, who enjoy the advantages common to both in a still higher degree.

22. From all these considerations it may perhaps appear that the best, plainest, and most effectual plan which any government can pursue for increasing the happiness and the numbers of its people is to increase the number of independent cultivators, to facilitate their establishments, and to bring into that favourable situation as great a number of citizens as the extent of its territory

will admit. Of two nations equal in extent of territory and in number of citizens, that may be accounted the happiest in which the number of independent cultivators is the greatest.

23. Any given country will then have the greatest possible number of independent cultivators, when each individual of mature age shall be possessed of an equal share of the soil; and in such country the common measure or standard of happiness will probably have reached its highest degree.

Whether therefore we inquire into the natural rights and privileges of men, or consult for the best interests of the greater number, the same practical regulations for the economy of property in land seem to result from either inquiry.

24. Whatsoever plans seem to promise the increase of wealth, happiness, and numbers in any other channel than the freedom and independence of cultivation, are of a more doubtful nature, and may well have their claim to public encouragement postponed until this paramount object of good policy be carried to its utmost perfection.

25. Manufactures and commerce promise such augmentation of wealth and people. Some degree of both is requisite for the progress of agriculture, and must attend it; but neither of them can in any situation of things have any title to encouragement at the risk of obstructing independent agriculture. The balance of their respective claims may always be adjusted in the most unexceptionable manner, by leaving men wholly to their free choice, and removing all obstruction and monopoly equally from the pursuit of both. Let all freedom be given to him who has stock, to employ it in any sort of trade, manufacture, or agriculture, that he may choose; and let it be made equally easy for the farmer to acquire the full property of the soil on which he is to exercise his industry, as for the manufacturer to acquire the full property of the rude materials he is to work up.

26. That every field should be cultivated by its proprietor, is most favourable to agriculture, and cultivation. That every individual who would choose it should be the proprietor of a field, and employed in its cultivation, is most favourable to happiness, and to virtue. In the combination of both circumstances will be found the most consummate prosperity of a people and of their country, and the best plan for accommodating the original right of universal occupancy with the acquired rights of labour...

SECTION VII. *Of a progressive Agrarian Law, while might be made the basis of all partial and occasional Reformation respecting Property in Land.*

71. If in any nation of Western Europe the sovereign were desirous of introducing a system of property in land, wholly consonant to natural justice, and favourable to the greatest happiness of the greatest number of citizens; and if in this undertaking he found himself under no necessity of paying respect to the prejudices and interests of the present landholders, or any other body of men whatever, he would take for his leading object to increase the number of independent cultivators, and to bring into that favourable situation as great a number of citizens as the extent of his territory would admit. In the accomplishment of which purpose, he might see cause to enact a statute, not very different from the plan delineated in the following articles:

I. That every citizen aged twenty-one years or upwards may, if not already in possession of land, be entitled to claim from the public a certain portion, not exceeding forty acres, to be assigned him in perpetuity for residence and cultivation, in the manner and under the conditions hereafter specified.

II. That the claimant shall have right to choose the situation of his allotment on any farm, freehold, or uncultivated common within his own parish, if the same be not excepted by the other provisions of this law. If there be no unexcepted land in his own parish, he shall have right to choose in any of the parishes contiguous to his own; and if in these there be no unexcepted land, he shall have right to choose throughout the whole district or county.

III. This allotment shall be set apart, and its landmarks fixed by the magistrate with the aid of an assize, or of arbitrators chosen by the parties. It shall be marked out in the manner most convenient for both the old and new occupier: it shall approach to a square, or some other compact form; one of its sides shall run along the boundary of the old farm; and it shall have communication with some road already patent. —None of these circumstances to be departed from without the consent of both parties.

IV. The ground thus set apart shall be submitted to the cognizance of an assize, or of arbitrators chosen by the parties, who shall determine what reserved perpetual rent the claimant must pay to the landlord, and what temporary rent to the former tenant (if any) in compensation of their rights.

V. The following farms are to be exempted from all such claims: —(1) Every farm from which, if the allotment claimed is taken away, less than forty acres will remain to the first tenant. (2) The farm or park belonging to the lord of the manor, the same bearing a regulated proportion only to the extent of his estate. (3) Every farm, of whatever extent, that has not been ten years occupied by the present tenant. (4) Every farm whose arable ground has been diminished one-half by claims founded on this law shall be exempted for twenty years to come, if the tenant so desire. (5) All farms of barren ground taken for the sake improvement, under such forms and limitations as may prevent the collusive evasion of this law.

VI. In case the claimant is not contented with the rent affixed to his allotment, he shall not be obliged to hold it, but to pay the occupier twice the amount of any expenses incurred by him. If the former occupier is not contented, a new valuation may be obtained by him, he defraying all the expenses that may attend it. Every such claimant may make four options, and no more. If he has made two within his own parish without holding, he cannot make a third there, but may make his remaining two in the contiguous parishes, or in the district at large, as he shall choose.

VII. The person thus acquiring property shall continue to reside upon his farm. He shall have right to transmit it to his heirs or assignees in full property, or under a reserved rent, but shall not have nor transmit the right of alienating it with reversion, *i.e.*, of letting it, or any part of it, in lease. If he sells it to another, who shall not reside upon, but annex it to some other farm, one-tenth part of the price, or of the reserved rent, shall belong to the public.

VIII. The lands acquired in this manner shall not be transmitted by will, but according to the established rules of succession to landed property, the original lord of the manor being *ultimus heres*. The father, however, may choose to which of his sons the farm shall devolve.

IX. No allotment shall be united to another by succession. The person who has right to two in this way shall make choice of one of them, and that which he relinquishes shall pass to the next heir. By marriage they may be united during the lives of the parties, and of the longest liver, but to be separately inherited by two of their heirs.

X. It shall not be lawful to break down any such allotment in order to divide it among children, until in any county the uncultivated lands are wholly exhausted; at which time, a new standard of farms shall take place, of six or eight acres, suited to the spade culture; and allotments within that county may then be broken down by will, purchase, or otherwise to that standard.

XI. The property acquired in these allotments shall not carry along with it any right of common of any sort in the commons, moors, woodlands, private roads, or other appendages of the manor, excepting only in the nearest well and watering pond, and in the bog or common for turf, if that is the fuel of the country: this last right to be regulated by the usages of the manor, as if the allotment had been given off in lease only. Neither shall any use, prescription, or connivance, ever in course of time, procure the holder of such allotment any right of common that is not founded on, and ascertained by, express compact.

XII. Those who are in possession of farms at the time of enacting this law shall not be entitled to get any part of their farms converted into freehold by its operation, until by the option of other claimants these farms be reduced to an extent of less than sixty acres.

XIII. All who acquire property by the operation of this law shall be obliged to perform double service in the militia of their country.

XIV. In every competition that may arise, orphans, and those that have served in the army or navy, shall be preferred to all others, and to one another according to the number of years they have served, or the early age at which they have been left orphans.

XV. Every person who has acquired an allotment of land in this manner shall pay to the lord of the manor certain aids and services of a feudal nature, so regulated as to produce that degree of connection and dependence which may be expedient for preserving order and subordination in the country without danger of giving rise to oppression and abuse.

72. Such might be the general outlines of a statute which from the nature of its operation would not improperly be called a progressive Agrarian law. Other more simple plans might no doubt be adopted by a sovereign having the power and the inclination above supposed. Many such might be proposed, by any of which the present state of landed property in Europe might be very much improved, and rendered more consistent with natural justice and the best interests of the greater number; yet far less improved than might be expected from the establishment of a

progressive Agrarian law, the plan of which seems to comprehend the following advantages over every other Agrarian law that has been attempted or proposed.

(1.) It tends to unite the real benefits of that leveling scheme which was the avowed object of the Greek and Roman Agrarian laws, and which the peasants of Europe, in a frenzy excited by oppression, have sometimes seemed to aim at; with the known advantages of unequal fortunes, and the free accumulation of real property, excluding at the same time the greater evils that attend on each.

(2.) That its operation must proceed gradually and gently, under the regulation of two principles, the one acting as an accelerating force, viz., the demand of the lower ranks for independent settlements, the other acting as a retarding or restraining force, viz., the inconvenience which the present occupiers, at any given period of time, must undergo. The opposite interests of these two classes of men, this law tends to compromise on a plan the least unjust to the former, and the least incommodious to the latter, according to the circumstances of the country at every successive point of time, with all the variations of which circumstances the operation of this law will, of course, vary.

(3.) That it provides for the easy gratification of that propensity so natural to mankind, to fix their settlements as near as may be to the places of their birth, and to extend themselves *de vicino de vicinum*, chiefly like the trees of the forest.

(4.) That it reduces no citizen to the alternative of renouncing his inclination or his right. If he does not incline to become a cultivator, or a husbandman, he is not therefore deprived of all opportunity of becoming so, when change of circumstances, or of his choice, shall so dispose him; when that time comes, he has free admission to an equal share of the soil of his country. Provision, however, is made, that whoever in the meantime has occupied that share shall not be dispossessed of it, with any circumstances of inconvenience, nor without a just compensation for labour bestowed and improvements made. In order to ascertain the amount of this compensation, recourse is had to the best expedient which the state of human affairs will permit, an expedient which in similar cases has been employed and found adequate.

(5.) That it may be so adjusted as to confer suitable and effectual encouragement on the marriages and increasing progeny of the lower classes of men; not merely honours, exemptions, and prizes, which can fall only to the share of a few, but real establishments proportioned to their increasing wants, and consisting of the subject of industry and the means of subsistence.

(6.) That by very easy variations it may be accommodated in a great measure to the municipal laws of any country, and the interests of any prevailing order of men, so as that very considerable and important branches of it, if not the whole, may be engrafted on the established system, whatever that may be, without any apparent violence or much danger of exciting discontent...

75. Still, it must be acknowledged that after setting aside all objections arising from the interest of landholders, and the prejudices of established opinion, there are not wanting others of a general nature which may be opposed, and not without some appearance of foundation, to the establishment of a progressive Agrarian law. That uncertain and fluctuating state into which all possession of land beyond the standard farm will be thrown, may be apprehended to prove extremely unfavourable to any spirited and vigorous cultivation, which is chiefly to be looked for in extensive farms. In the plan of a progressive Agrarian, more than one clause is calculated to moderate this fluctuation; greater force may be given to these, and new clauses of corresponding effect may be added. It might be provided, for example, that none but barren and uncultivated lands should be open to claimants at all times; cultivated lands only one year in seven, or any longer period that may be thought requisite for the security of cultivation; neither indeed ought uncertainty of possession to damp very much the spirit of improvement, while the improver is still secure of an adequate reward for the pains he may have taken; and that reward is to be assigned him by the verdict of an assize; at the worst, in proportion as the spirit of improvement may be damped in extensive farms, it will be encouraged and excited in the smaller, where possession and full property is rendered secure; and in these, improvements being carried on under the immediate continual inspection, and almost by the hands of the improver himself, they will be accomplished with more economy, that is, with more advantage to the public and to individuals than commonly happens in extensive undertakings of this sort.

The discouragement of established manufactures and the increase of litigious contention are in like manner objections which must be admitted to a certain extent, yet not to that degree as to be accounted national calamities, or to equiponderate the obvious and great advantages likely to arise from a due regulation of landed property.

It cannot be supposed that any great number of men, educated to manufactures and accustomed to the practice of mechanic arts, will be withdrawn from their respective trades, even by the free opportunities of engaging in independent agriculture; but a competition will take place with respect to the rising progeny of the present race, and if the greater number shall attach themselves to agriculture, it need not be regarded as any detriment to the public, since, the number of citizens remaining the same, they will be employed in a way which they themselves prefer, and probably to the advantage of their health and of their manners.

With whatever violence the increase of litigation may break forth in consequence of regulations so new, so important, and not a little complicated, the duration of that evil cannot be very lasting. In a few years doubtful cases will be cleared up, and precedents of extensive application will be established, and whilst the attention of judicatories and of clients is engaged in settling these new points, the influence of other causes by which litigation is commonly produced will be in some degree suspended.

As for the beneficial effects of such a statute, the candid and intelligent are requested to estimate in their own thoughts what these might prove in the district with which they are most particularly acquainted, and to consider whether it would not very much improve the condition and the prospects of the day labourer, the hired servant, and the working manufacturer, without imposing on the established farmer or the landlord any unjust or even any considerable inconvenience? Whether it would not lessen the number of the indigent and the idle, and so reduce the rate of that tax by which the rich are obliged to maintain them? Whether it would not tend to promote cultivation and the fertility of the soil, to favour the increase of population, and to improve the manners and virtues of the great body of the people? After having made this estimate, let them consider what might have been the present state of that district had such a progressive Agrarian law or any capital branch of that statute been established there one hundred or even fifty years ago.

Seven

Thomas Reid
(1710–1796)

SOME THOUGHTS ON THE UTOPIAN SYSTEM
(1794)

There are two Questions in politics which are perfectly distinct, and which ought never to be confounded. The first is, What is that form or order of political society which, abstractly considered, tends most to the improvement and happiness of man?

The second question is, how may a form of government which actually exists and has been long established be changed, and reduced to a form which we think more eligible?

The second question is difficult in speculation and very dangerous in practice; dangerous, not only to those who attempt it but to the society in general.

Every change of government is either sudden and violent, or it (is) gradual, peaceable and legal.

A violent change of government, considering the means that must be used to effect it, and the uncertainty of the issue, must be an object of dread to every wise, and every humane man.

It is to wrest power from the hands of those who are possessed of it, in the uncertain hope of our being able, and the more uncertain hope that, after a violent convulsion, it shall fall into hands more to our mind.

The means of effecting such a change are plots, conspiracies, sedition, rebellion, civil war, bloodshed and massacre in which the innocent and the guilty promiscuously suffer.

If we should even suppose that a total and sudden change of government could be produced without those violent means; that by a miracle those in power and office should voluntarily lay down their authority, and leave a nation to choose a new form of government; Suppose also that, by another miracle, foreign enemies should not take the advantage of this state of anarchy. What would be the consequence?

A very small state, like an ancient Greek city, when they banished their tyrant, might meet and consult for the common good. The issue of this consultation commonly was, to choose a wise and disinterested man, who was superior to themselves in political knowledge, and to give him power to model a government for them. And this was perhaps the wisest method they could take. For a good model of government can never, all at once, be invented by a multitude, of which the greater part is ignorant, and of the knowing, the greater part is led by interest or by ambition.

A great nation however cannot meet together to consult. They must therefore have deputies chosen by different districts. But previous to this, the number and limits of the districts, the qualifications of the electors and candidates and the form and method of election must be ascertained. How these preliminaries are to be fixed when all authority is dissolved and the nation in a state of anarchy, is a question I am not able to resolve.

Supposing however this difficult point to be happily settled, and the electors of a district met to choose a deputy. Is it to be supposed that all or the greater part of those electors are to be determined by a pure and disinterested regard to the good of the nation? He surely knows little of human nature who would admit such a supposition. We know from long experience how such elections proceed. The poor electors must have their bellies or their purses filled, their burdens lessened or their superiors mollified. The rich must have their private attachments and friendships gratified, or good deeds done, or promised or expected. There may no doubt be electors who are both knowing and perfectly disinterested, but the proportion they bear to the whole, I am afraid is too small to be brought into estimation.

Such being the electors, who are to be candidates? It were to be wished that they should be the wisest and the best men of the district. But this is rather to be wished than expected. It is evident they must be men who have it in their power and in their inclination to offer the inducements by which a majority may be gained. Without this their pretensions would be laughed at.

To pass over these things, suppose an assembly of deputies met, and a constitution of government determined, unanimously or by a majority. Whether this constitution is to be imposed upon the nation by a despotic authority of the deputies, or to be again submitted to the choice of the people, I cannot pretend to determine, nor shall I enumerate the dangers that may arise from the one of these ways or the other. After all the favourable Suppositions I have made, it seems to me that to bring such a government to a firm and settled condition must be the work of a century.

For we may observe that the stability of a government, if it be at all tolerable, depends greatly upon its antiquity. Customs and manners by which we and our forefathers for many generations have been governed, acquire an authority and a sanctity independent upon their reasonableness or utility. To this disposition of human nature, I think it is owing, rather than to climate or to any peculiarity in the genius of the people, that very imperfect forms of government, when by a mild administration they have continued for many generations, and acquired the authority of antiquity, continue to subsist after they become very tyrannical. When intolerable grievances are felt that produce sedition, they are imputed, not to the form of government, but to the fault of those who administer it. Thus in Turkey, a sedition is quelled by the sacrifice of a vizier, a mufti, or sometimes of a sultan, without any attempt to alter the form of government. Into this reverence for the ancient form of government I think we must likewise resolve that maxim, admitted by all political writers, that when an ancient government is overturned, either by conquest or by internal disorder, the safest way to establish a new one, is to keep as much as possible to the old forms of procedure and the old names of offices.

What I have said hitherto relates to violent and sudden changes of the form of government, and the conclusion from the whole is, that such changes are so dangerous in the attempt, so uncertain in the issue, and so dismal and destructive in the means by which they are brought about, that it must be a very bad form of government indeed, with circumstances very favourable to a change concurring, that will justify a wise and good man in putting a hand to them. It is not with an old government as with an old house, from which the inhabitant, who desires a new one, may remove with his family and goods till it be pulled down and rebuilt. If we pull down the old government, it must be pulled down about our ears, and we must submit to the danger of having the new built over our heads.

But there may be changes that are not sudden and violent, but gradual peaceable and legal. New laws and ordinances wisely contrived may remedy the defects of a constitution, remove grievances, and promote general happiness.

This must be granted; Yet so limited is the wisdom of man, so short his foresight, that new laws, even when made with the best intention, do not always produce the effect intended and expected from them, or they bring unforseen inconveniences that do more than counterbalance their good effects. For this reason even such changes ought not to be rashly made, but with good advice and for weighty causes.

Surely every man who has the skill and ability to mend the constitution by such peaceable means merits the blessings of a nation. And every constitution, in proportion as it gives scope for such amendments, by allowing due liberty of printing and petitioning, and by giving the people a share in the legislature, is in the way of having its defects supplied and its errors corrected.

We have the comfort to think that in this respect as in many others the British constitution excels all others we know.

The change made at the revolution in 1688 was violent indeed but necessary. It affected only one branch of the legislature, and by the good providence of God was brought about with fewer of the evils that commonly attend such revolutions than could have reasonably been expected. Since that time, we have had no revolution, but such gradual and peaceable changes, by new laws, as have improved the constitution and greatly promoted the prosperity of the nation; and it is to be hoped we may long continue to have such.

*

Having said so much with regard to changes in governments which actually exist, whether violent or peaceable I proceed to what I chiefly intended in this discourse: To consider abstractly that form of political society which seems to be best adapted to the improvement and happiness of man.

This is a point merely speculative. For it may be that the form which in speculation seems best fitted to the end proposed may be impracticable in a particular nation or even in any nation that exists.

Man, who is the subject of all political discussion whether speculative or practical, may be considered in two views. In the first he is the subject of speculative politics, in the second of practical. First he may be considered ... such as nature has formed him, a being who brings into the world with him the seeds of reason and conscience, along with various appetites and passions, by which he is often misled into error, and seduced into wrong conduct by temptations that arise from within, or from external circumstances: At the same time capable of a high degree of improvement in knowledge and virtue, by right education and good government; and on the other hand, of great degeneracy, to barbarity and even to brutality, by the want or the corruption of these means. This is the man of nature, the subject of speculative politics, and the subject of what is to be said in this discourse. The practical politician, who is to model or to direct the government of a nation actually existing, has to do with men who are not in the state of nature, but who by education and by the state of society in which they live have acquired habits and dispositions, which it is not in his power to eradicate, and which may be called a second nature. To this second nature as well as to the first his principles of government must be adapted.

If it be asked, to what purpose it is to turn our attention to points merely speculative and visionary? I answer that speculative points ought not to be excluded from the circle of human knowledge. They tend to enlarge our conceptions and to strengthen our faculties. Speculation has a like effect with regard to our intellectual powers as bodily exercises have, with regard to the health strength and agility of the body. Besides, when political discussions have come to be so much in fashion among all ranks, it may perhaps be as profitable to most men, to employ their thoughts upon what is merely speculative, as upon what may influence their practice.

It were to be wished that the conduct of men in society was directed uniformly by the principles of religion and virtue; but this is not to be expected, and if it were, there would be no need of civil government. The materials of the political fabric are men, not such as they ought to be, but such as they are, made up of reason and passion, of virtue and vice. The state of human nature is such that to produce happiness and comfort in human society, the principles of virtue and religion need the aid and cooperation of other principles of an inferior order, which shall have sufficient influence to restrain men from wrong conduct, and induce them to do what is right.

Wrong conduct is always owing either to error or judgment, or some temptation which leads men to do what they know to be wrong. If there be any so very corrupt as to do mischief for mischief's sake, without any temptation, they are not fit to be members of society, and can only be objects of restraint and punishment.

From this it follows that in an enlightened society, crimes will bear proportion to the number and greatness of temptations, and that the least of ill conduct will be found in a society in which the minds of the citizens are properly enlightened in their duty, and have at the same time the least temptation to do ill.

But to the happiness of society it is not sufficient that men do no ill; they must do good; and by their industry and activity promote the common stock of happiness.

To aid the principles of virtue and religion in exciting men to that industry and activity which the happiness of society requires, the love of public esteem, honour and rank seems, of all the inferior principles of human nature, to be the best adapted. It is by far a more generous and noble principle than the love of money or of private interest. It is also more allied to virtue. A man may acquire riches by means honest or dishonest, but to acquire esteem his conduct must be accounted honest and laudable. Esteem is the natural reward of merit, and so strong is the natural desire of it in all men, that if every man's merit or demerit were publicly known, and if he were to carry about with him through life and to leave at his death, a degree of public esteem or contempt proportioned to it, we can hardly conceive a man so degenerate, as not to be moved to industry and activity in his station by so powerful an incitement.

From what has been said I think we may in general conclude that the best form of political society is that in which these three things concur. First, that the most effectual means be used to strengthen in the minds of the citizens the principles of virtue and true religion and to enlighten them in what is right and wrong, honourable and dishonourable. Secondly, that the temptations to wrong and criminal conduct be as few as possible. And thirdly, that public esteem, honour and rank be proportioned as exactly as possible to real merit.

If this be so, political knowledge as far as it is speculative, must be the knowledge of the means by which these three ends may be most effectually accomplished.

As to the first, the means of enlightening the people in what is right and wrong and strengthening in their minds the principles of true religion and virtue, though I conceive it to be a point of very high importance with regard to political government, yet it has been so often treated of, with regard to a higher end, to wit the happiness of men in another world, that I shall pass over it altogether, lest I should seem to degrade religion by considering it as an engine of state.

I proceed therefore to consider in what state or order of society there is least temptation to ill conduct, and I confess that to me the utopian system of Sir Thomas More seems to have the advantage of all others in this respect.

In that system, it is well known there is no private property. All that which we call *property* is under the administration of the state for the common benefit of the whole political family.

This government indeed very much resembles that of a single family, which is the only government that can be said to be purely the institution of nature, all others that exist being artificial and the contrivance of men.

It is the appointment of nature, that man should subsist by labour, and to the comfortable subsistence of a nation, a certain quantity and kind of labour is necessary. By this labour, almost all that which we call property is produced; and there are two ways in which this labour may be regulated. Either every man labours for himself and his family, as his necessity and desire prompt him, and is proprietor of the produce of his own labour; Or, every man labours for the whole nation, the produce of his labour being put to the common stock from which every citizen is supplied according to his wants.

The first we may call the system of private property, which is exemplified in all nations. The second is the utopian system which as far as we know has not been followed by any great nation. It has been practiced in different ages by societies of cenobites and monks who have lived sequestered from the world, by the labour of their own hands. It was practiced by our Saviour and his twelve apostles who had a common purse during his ministry on earth; and after his ascension, the first christians had all things in common, they that had lands or houses sold them and laid the price at the apostles' feet, and distribution was made to every man as he had need. After the christians amounted to a multitude consisting of several thousands, the seven deacons were chosen to manage and distribute this common stock. And it was probably their dispersion into different countries, by the persecution of the Jews, that put an end to this community of property among christians.

This system was also established by some Jesuits, over a large tract of country in Paraguay, which by good deeds and without force they brought from a savage state under their despotic authority. The Jesuits who governed this country with a mild but despotic authority, carried on a large traffic to different parts of South America, and paid a piaster to the king of Spain for each of their subjects, amounting about the middle of this century as it is said to above four hundred thousand. But the subjects had neither money nor property nor traffic. This government of the Jesuits in Paraguay lasted about a hundred and fifty years, and ended only by the entire destruction of the Society of Jesuits.

In the utopian system the people are fed, clothed, and have their wants supplied by the public, the labour of the people must therefore be directed by the public, in such manner that the produce of it may be sufficient in kind and quantity for this purpose. The labourers in every profession must be trained, directed and overseen and the produce of their labour received and stored by proper officers.

The means by which this is to be done will be a subsequent consideration, but first we ought to consider whether the end be of importance to the happiness of society.

Suppose then a nation of which the individuals have all their wants supplied by the public, the produce of their labour being to be put to a public stock for the common benefit. I would endeavour to prove that in such a nation the temptations to wrong or criminal conduct would be small, compared with those which must happen in any system of private property.

It is a proverb of the highest authority that the love of money is the root of all evil. Like other proverbs it must be understood to admit of exceptions. But the truth of it, (which no Christian will deny) requires, that the exceptions should be few compared with the instances in which it holds good. There may, no doubt, be crimes which have no relation to the love of money. But by far the greater part of those we find in human society, spring either immediately or more remotely from this root. Nor will this appear strange if we consider how this root, when once admitted, spreads and infects the whole society. Let it be observed, by the way, that the words, property, money, and riches, may be used in this subject promiscuously as equivalent terms; because money is the measure of all property and all property may (be) bought or sold for its value in money. Riches signify only a superfluity of property either in money or in other kinds.

Next to the desire of life and of the necessary means of life; the desire of distinction and preeminence among his fellowmen is one of the strongest natural desires of man; and when his whole activity is not necessarily employed in providing the means of subsistence, is the strongest, the most general, and lasting spring of activity and exertion. Now riches, in all civilized societies, seem to have advantages above all other qualifications for gratifying this desire. For, first, in all such societies, riches are more looked up to than wisdom or virtue or learning or art, or any other qualification by which one man excels another.

Secondly, riches are the means of gratifying almost every desire. They are a species of power, which is a natural object of desire to all men. They may be equally subservient to the best purposes and to the worst, to the happiness or misery of the possessor and of many others. In bad men they feed pride, vanity, luxury, and voluptuousness; they invite to oppression and revenge and furnish the means of gratifying every bad passion. In good men they may be the means of doing much good.

Thirdly, riches and hereditary rank which commonly arises from riches and accompanies them are the only advantages which a man can transmit to his posterity or family.

Fourthly, we may observe that the acquisition of riches requires neither talents nor virtues, so that this road to distinction invites all men, even those who may despair of attaining it by other means.

I add in the last place, that though many of our passions may be satiated by their objects, and even surfeited; the love of money is never satiated. It grows in old age when other passions fade.

These particulars have been mentioned to show the reason why, when private property is once admitted, the desire and the pursuit of it, and consequently all the evils that spring from that root should be so universal, and so prevalent in society.

Indeed when we take a general view of society, What is it else but a scramble for money? In a few perhaps, who have inherited fortunes, it is a competition who shall make the most brilliant exhibition of riches by show and magnificence. Such is become the serious business of mankind in consequence of the system of private property!

The utopian system may be figured, by a sum of money prudently distributed to a great multitude according to their wants and their merits. The system of private property, to a like sum, thrown promiscuously among the same multitude leaving them to scramble for it.

Private property has always been, and must necessarily be very unequally divided. Time, and the progress of society, naturally tend to increase this inequality, till at last the greater part of a nation, by their poverty are depressed and dependent upon the few that are rich; they must labour, like beasts of burden, to feed the pride and luxury of the rich, and to earn a small pittance for their own necessary subsistence. By this means both are equally corrupted; the greater part being debased into a state of servility, which tends to stifle every generous sentiment, and to produce envy and discontent in all, adulation and cunning in the more timorous, and in the more daring, theft, robbery, murder, sedition and rebellion.

On the other hand the rich, being as much elevated above the natural condition of man, as the poor are sunk below it, and that commonly without regard to virtue or merit, are as much corrupted by their riches as the poor by their poverty. It is unnecessary to enumerate the vices to which riches tempt the unprincipled; they are obvious to reason and well known by experience.

Nor is it less evident that the distinction attending upon riches very much diminishes the inducement which such persons would otherwise feel to distinguish themselves by more valuable qualities.

For, among the evils which may justly be imputed to the system of private property, this is not the least, that the strong desire which all men have of distinction and eminence, which naturally excites them to honourable and useful conduct in society, and is implanted in us by the supreme being for that purpose, is perverted to the love of money, as the easiest and surest road to distinction.

In the system of private property every man has his private interest, distinct, not only from the public interest, but from the interest of every individual with whom he has any connection or intercourse. There is an interest of every individual and an interest of the whole political body. These different interests must in innumerable cases interfere, and cross one another. And the public interest crosses that of every individual, because the public must be supported at the expense of the individuals.

From this opposition of interests arise disaffection to the public, discontent, contentions, parties, and law pleas, by which all the bad passions of men are stirred, and fed. And in the same proportion public spirit and all the natural benevolent affections are checked, opposed and born down.

In the utopian system there are no private interests opposed to that of the public. A regard to the public acts without an antagonist; nor is there any clashing of private interests to produce quarrels and lawsuits. The benevolent affections have no interested motives to obstruct their operation.

I know of no temptations to bad conduct that are peculiar to the utopian system; deducing therefore those that are common to both systems the balance against that of private property consists of all the temptations which occur in an enlightened and flourishing nation, in the acquisition of property, in guarding it from the encroachments of other men, and in spending and laying it out. The temptations from poverty in the greater part arise from the greedy desire of gain in some, and from superfluity of riches in others.

I grant that notwithstanding the temptations mentioned men guided by the principles of virtue and piety may acquire property by fair and honest means, and without hurt to the public may guard it prudently and peaceably, and lay it out temperately and charitably. But in all political reasoning we must consider, not what men may do, or what they ought to do, but what it may be expected they will do in the present weak and corrupted state of human nature. We see in our daily experience that temptations of interest overcome, not only the sense of duty, but the natural good affections to neighbours, to friends, to the nearest relations and even to the public.

From what has been said I think it appears that the utopian system is that in which there are fewest temptations to bad conduct. I proceed therefore to consider whether in this system, men may not have sufficient inducement to all the labour and exertion necessary to the subsistence and happiness of the society by degrees of public esteem, honour and rank proportioned to their merit.

With a view to this, it is absolutely necessary, that the right education of all the subjects, should be attended to by the state, as one of its principal concerns; and should be under the direction of persons qualified for that office, and having a degree of rank and public esteem, suited to the dignity and importance of their charge.

It is education generally that makes a man to be what he is; not only knowing or ignorant, but good or bad. For this we have the authority of another proverb: train up a child in the way he should go, and when he is old he will not depart from it.

What more can be desired in order to the greatest happiness of society, than that its members, in their several departments, should go on to old age in the way they ought to go? The proper means to attain this end, in the judgment of the wisest of men is to train them properly. Until this be done, it is in vain to expect from any system of government, that perfection and happiness of society which every good man desires. The materials of the political fabric must be formed to fit the places for which they are destined.

Without this there can neither be beauty nor stability in the building.

It seems to be a natural consequence of the system of private property, that the education of the youth in all nations (if we except what is said of one or two very ancient ones) has been left to the judgment and affection of the parents. And as the far greatest part of parents in every nation is poor and ignorant, it is a necessary consequence, that the education of the far greatest part of the citizens must be very different from what it ought to be; and that this most efficacious means of their acting a proper part in society has been wanting.

In a utopian government, as the labour and exertion of the citizens is all for the public emolument, it must be one of the most important concerns of the public to train them properly for that purpose.

So much has been written upon education in ancient and modern times, that I shall not touch on that subject. I would only observe, that to teach men to read and write, the use of numbers, and the various exercises that contribute to the health strength and agility of the body, and even to Latin, Greek, Mathematics and the various branches of philosophy, and to instruct them in the principles of any particular science or art useful in society; all this, however skillfully performed, is but the body of right education. These attainments are all of an ambiguous nature, and may be used either to the good or to the hurt of society, according to the character of him who possesses them. And therefore, to form the character to good habits and good dispositions, and to check those that are vicious; this is the soul and spirit of right education. To accomplish this as far as can be done by human means, requires great knowledge of human nature, constant attention, great temper, patience and assiduity. The diseases of the mind while it is pliable and docile as well as those of the body may, by prudent means, be cured or alleviated.

Those who superintend education in a utopian society, ought to be men who by their merit have attained public respect and honour; which may give authority to their admonitions, and make them examples worthy to be imitated by those under their care. And, as nature has not made the talents of body or mind that are useful in society, hereditary, or peculiar to any rank; the symptoms of such talents in whatever rank ought to be carefully observed and cultivated, that they may in due time be put to their proper use.

There is an education that ought to be common to all the citizens; such as may enlighten their minds in the duties of life, and dispose them to the practice of them. Another education must follow this, suited to the different employments for which the young citizens are destined, according to their various talents of body and mind, and as the public exigency requires.

As the labour in every employment is for the public, it must be overseen by officers appointed by the public, who shall at stated times make a report to superior officers of the industry, skill and moral behaviour of every individual under their charge.

It is a capital defect in the system of private property that the different professions and employments are not honoured and esteemed in proportion to their real utility, and the talents required for the discharge of them. The most useful and necessary employments are held in no esteem. Nor indeed do they deserve it; because they are undertaken only for the sake of private interest. Their utility to the public is accidental, and not in the view of those who practice them. It is otherwise in a utopian state where every man labours in his calling, not for his own, but for the public benefit. He is therefore justly entitled to public esteem in proportion to the utility the public receives from his labour and the difficulty of performing it.

In such a society, there must be a scale of honour in which all the different professions and employments have a rank assigned them, proportioned to their utility and the talents necessary for discharging them. There must likewise be distinctive badges or habits, by which every man's rank and the respect due to him may be known and observed in all cases of precedency.

And, as in every profession and employment there will be different degrees of eminence and proficiency these ought, in a utopian system, to be used as a spur to emulation and exertion. If in the literary professions, the degrees of undergraduate, bachelor, licentiat and doctor be found useful to excite to industry in those professions, why may not like degrees for every employment be appointed? In a utopian society this ought by no means to be omitted. As in that form of society, next to the principle of virtue, the desire of public esteem and honour is the grand spring which gives motion to the whole machine of the commonwealth, it is proper that there should (be) many roads to public honours, that every man in his station may be prompted to exert himself for the public good.

For this cause besides the kinds and degrees of public honours I have mentioned, there ought to be an order of merit for those who have remarkably benefited the commonwealth in any way not comprehended in these I have mentioned, which also will have various degrees. If we add to this the honours and dignities arising from offices of trust and authority in the state, which must be many, and of different degrees; it will appear, that in such a state there will be a much greater variety of ranks than in any other; and these distinguished, not by riches or hereditary descent, which are distinctions not founded in nature but on human institution; but distinguished in a more natural way, by their talents natural and acquired, by their exertions for the public good, and by the authority and trust they have merited of their fellow citizens.

Luxury and intemperance in eating and drinking are pernicious in every state, and in a system of private property can hardly if at all be prevented. How they are prevented in a utopian state is so obvious that it need not be mentioned. The subsistence of all ought to be such as leads to health and strength, and therefore most liberal to those whose labour requires it. Nature seems to point to no other difference among citizens in this article.

But there is a splendor and magnificence, in having servants, horses, chariots, houses and furniture, which does not appear to me to be incompatible with the utopian state, though Sir Thomas More seems to be of another mind.

When such splendor is bestowed by the state, as the reward of merit, either in a man's life or at his death; it is the most substantial reward such a state can give, and proves an incentive to merit in others, as well as creates respect in the lower orders.

On the other hand, when splendor and magnificence is produced merely by riches without regard to merit, it feeds pride and insolence in the possessor, inflames the love of money in those who can acquire it, and produces envy and malignity in those who cannot.

When I speak of servants in the utopian state, the word seems to convey a degrading idea of dependence, unsuitable to the dignity of a citizen of utopia, and therefore we should rather call them attendants or retainers. When a utopian of rank is allowed more or fewer attendants either for honour or for useful purposes, they are the servants of the state as he likewise is, though of a higher rank. They depend not upon the person whom they attend, but upon the state and upon their own merit for their subsistence and for their reward, and he has the same dependence. They have all the privileges that belong to citizens of utopia, and therefore are not degraded by such attendance.

What I have said is intended to show that every citizen of utopia, being properly educated, may, without the motive of private interest, have sufficient inducement to exert himself in his station for the public good, by being secured in liberal subsistence, and in such degrees of public esteem, honour and rank as are proportioned to his merit.

But if after all some persons should be found so degenerate, as that either their laziness and indolence, or other vicious inclinations, are not to be overcome by these inducements; the utopian state has a means in reserve for such persons; and that is dishonour and disgrace; of which a man may be made to carry about with him the marks, as others do of their dignity and honour.

Supposing the nature of some so very bad, that neither the motives of honour, nor of disgrace, are sufficient to make them act their part in society, penal laws and punishment, as in other states, are still in reserve for them, and in the utopian state ought to be applied to them only. Such persons have the temper of slaves, and ought to be degraded into that state; being altogether unworthy and incapable of being citizens of utopia.

It is obvious that in a utopian state the subjects can have no traffic either with one another or with foreigners; but the state may be commercial. It may be so with great advantage; having the whole stock of the nation in its disposal. And it ought to be so, that what, in the produce of the nation's industry is over and above its consumption, may be disposed of to other nations or individuals for its value and that the utopians may be supplied with such foreign commodities as are necessary or convenient.

A utopian state ought, by frugal management of the public stock, and by proper incitements to the industry and labour of the subjects, to be always provided in ample stores and a rich treasury, by which not only the annual consumption of the citizens may be supplied, but an accumulating fund may be reserved for foreign traffic, for the expense of defensive wars, for accidental losses by unfruitful seasons, inundations, earthquakes or tempests, and by unforeseen variations in commercial affairs.

When the loss of property occasioned by such evils falls only upon a public stock which is able to bear it, and affects no individual, every man may imagine what a comfort it must be to a nation, to be free from the fears and from the sufferings produced in other nations by such calamities. A utopian has every thing that pertains to his subsistence, and to his rank in the society, insured upon the stock and credit of the nation, against all accidents, excepting that of his own misbehaviour. He fears no loss of fortune or of consideration by fire or water or any other element, by insolvency of debtors or of tenants, or by depredations of enemies foreign or domestic.

It may seem that in this system, the state is burdened with a load of work, additional to the common cares of government, too great to be well accomplished. The education of all the youth of both sexes, the oversight of all the labouring hands, the collecting, storing and dispensing the produce of their labour, the public registers that must be kept of the merits and demerits of every individual, and of every step of his advancement in honour and rank, the regulations for conferring degrees with justice and impartiality, and the management of the trading stock of the nation, these things, without doubt, will require much attention and fidelity, and many hands.

To form an equitable judgment of a utopian government in this respect, it would be necessary to balance these additional burdens that are laid upon it, with those of which it is relieved; and likewise with those of which the subjects are relieved; for as government and subjects are one whole, having one common interest, what is taken from one part and laid upon another part, does not increase the burden of the whole.

In this system, government is relieved of all the care and trouble of imposing and levying taxes of customs excise and all others, affecting either moveable or immoveable property, and of all the hands employed for that purpose, and for preventing and discovering the frauds which citizens are tempted to by private interest and avarice, in opposition to the public interest.

In a system of private property taxes of all kinds though necessary for the support of government, are attended with this inconvenience, that they set the interest of the whole in opposition to the interest of the individuals, which is apt to produce disaffection to the public, sedition and rebellion, and will always be attended with smuggling, frauds, and concealments which corrupt the morals of the citizens and produce innumerable law pleas.

To manage the whole traffic of a nation is, no doubt, a business of great labour, and must require the employment of many hands in its various subordinate departments. But it is to be considered whether one great mercantile stock may not be managed better, and more profitably for the nation, than when it is divided into thousands of different stocks, of companies and individuals, whose private interests must in innumerable cases cross one another, and that of the public.

The right education of the youth is a matter of such high importance in a utopian state, that if it should require more or abler hands than are commonly employed in it, this will be more than compensated by its effects on the manners and morals of the citizens.

The regulations for conferring, with justice and impartiality, degrees of honour and rank, fall within the rules of common prudence, as cases of this kind must happen more or less in every society. Only it may be observed that in utopia interested motives to partiality have no place. And that the character and behaviour of candidates, their skill, exertion and merit, must be perfectly known, from the particular inspection they are under.

The registers kept in utopia of the reports of overseers, and of the degrees of honour and advancement conferred on every citizen, furnish the government with a fund of statistical knowledge of great importance, which could not otherwise be had. From these are known the strength or weakness, the defects and redundancies of the whole political body, and of every part of it. If there be a deficiency of any article of life in the whole, or in any part from unfruitful seasons or any other accident; it will be known in time to provide a supply. If a redundancy, it will be stored or exported to a market. A defect or redundancy of hands in any employment may be corrected. Any useful invention or improvement is not kept a secret by the inventor for his private interest, or confined to the knowledge of a small neighbourhood, but is immediately made known to the whole nation. The persons fit for offices of trust and government will be known, and such offices filled, not by intrigue or connection with great men, as is common, but according to the public judgment of their capacity and merit.

It may farther be observed that if a utopian government be burdened with much work in its executive branch it is relieved of a great deal in its legislative and judiciary branches.

> 1st The laws relating to customs excise and other internal taxes; the judicatures superior and subordinate which are appointed to put those laws in execution, and all the pleas between government and subjects to which they give occasion, have no place in utopia.
>
> 2^{ly} All the laws and judicatures for determining pleas of interest between subject and subject, or between the subjects and foreigners, are likewise excluded in this system.

How great a body of law is required to regulate the acquisition, the conveyance, and the succession to landed property, its limits, its privileges, servitudes, and variety of holdings? And what a world of business does it occasion to judicatures higher and lower? How many the laws required to determine disputes about moveable property?

The variety of transactions which property gives rise to, is boundless and in an ancient and flourishing nation, is still accumulating, by new inventions, new trades, and new fashions, which give rise to new frauds and injuries, and require new laws.

Thus the body of laws, which the regulation of property, and the redress of wrongs in matters of property, require, is still accumulating, until it becomes too great a study for a life, and must be divided and subdivided into various professions and departments, and besides judicatures and judges, employs an host of counselors, advocates, sergeants, solicitors, conveyancers, clerks, registers, who are supported by what some of them have been pleased to call, the glorious uncertainty of law.

3dly We may observe, that as property is the chief bone of contention among mankind, by which the passions of anger and ill will are stirred and by which men are tempted to hurt one another in their person and reputation as well as property; in the utopian system, all contention about property being removed, and the fuel that feeds evil and malevolent passions being withdrawn; the evils which they produce in society will very rarely appear.

So that to compensate the labour laid upon the executive branch of a utopian government and the hands employed for that purpose, we ought to put in the other scale, the savings of labour and of hands in the legislative and judicative branches.

In the legislative branch is saved the labour of contriving and imposing the taxes of every kind necessary for the support of government, and the greater labour of making the laws for the regulation of property real and personal in the infinite variety of transactions civil and commercial that take place in society.

In the judicative branch is saved, the labour of judging and determining in all claims and pleas to be decided by those laws.

The saving of hands is likewise great in the utopian system, first to the government, of the hands necessary for the labour above mentioned in lawmaking and in judging; and secondly to the subjects of counselors, pleaders, conveyancers, and all their retainers whatsoever who are employed in the execution of the laws about property.

A third saving to the subjects, which is the greatest of all, is, that they are relieved of all the bitter fruits which spring, either immediately, or more remotely, from contentions and lawsuits about property.

One who considers these things can hardly forbear to conclude, that in a utopian state the code of law will be reduced to such a diminutive size, that it will hardly be thought worthy to be made a distinct profession. The law may be understood by common men come to years of discretion, and perhaps may be all contained in the almanac.

What I have said of the utopian system may be summed up in these three particulars: First, that the temptations to wrong and criminal conduct are by this system greatly diminished beyond what they must be in every system of private property.

Secondly, that by proper education, and by degrees of honour and rank conferred according to merit, the citizens of utopia may have sufficient inducement to all the labour and industry which is necessary to the comfortable subsistence of the nation. And thirdly, that the labour required in the executive branch of a utopian government is compensated by the labour of which it is relieved in the legislative and judicative branches; and much more by the subjects being relieved of all the bad passions, quarrels, contentions and lawsuits arising from differences about property.

The view I have hitherto taken of the utopian system presents its fairest side; to form an equitable judgement of it, it ought likewise to be contemplated on its darker side.

First it may be observed that political reasoning is not of the demonstrative but of the probable kind. The heart of man is a labyrinth, too intricate to be fully traced by his understanding and we often see, not only individuals, but great bodies of men act a part very different from that which by the common principles of human nature we would have expected. And therefore political writers are wont to borrow aid to their reasoning from examples of what has been done or has happened in similar cases. In the present subject, we are totally deprived of this adminicle to our reasoning; and therefore it must have the less force. We cannot borrow examples from utopian governments because no nation was ever so governed.

Secondly, as the present state of man is a state of trial and improvement, temptation is necessarily implied in it. It is by temptation that virtue is tried, exercised, and strengthened. That innocence, which is the effect of having never met with temptation, is, no doubt, a very amiable thing. But tried virtue which has encountered strong temptations, and has come off victorious, is an object of much higher esteem, both with god and man. Man even in the state of innocence was not exempted from temptation. Some have more or greater than others, but to what degree temptation may be proper for the present state of man, is not for us to know, it can only be known by him who made us, and who will judge us.

Thirdly, it may be observed that as the utopian system greatly lessens temptations to bad conduct, so it deprives men of the opportunity of exercising some very eminent virtues, to which the different conditions of poverty and riches give occasion. The man depressed by poverty, who not only resists the temptations of that state and discharges the duties of it, but is contented, and thankful for his lot as that which his father in heaven sees to be best for him, who looks with indifference upon the splendor of riches without a covetous eye, without envy or malignity; Such a man under all his depression carries a noble soul. His poverty exalts him, and makes his virtue more eminent. The temptations that arise from riches and high estate, are perhaps more difficult to be overcome than those which spring from poverty this is granted; and therefore they require a greater degree of virtue to conquer them. If such a man thinks of himself no more highly than he ought to think, condescends to those of low degree, spreads happiness and alleviates misery as far as his power reaches, he is a kind of god upon earth, his riches are a blessing to himself and to all around him.

The utopian system leaves no room for these noble virtues. The utopian may have the disposition but he wants the opportunity of exercising them.

I add in the fourth place that the desire of public esteem, honour and rank, which must be encouraged in the utopian system, as the chief aid to virtue for exciting men to do their duty in society, may be carried too far; so as to supplant the virtue which it ought only to aid. When this is the case the utopian indeed does his duty, but he does it, to be seen of men, when he ought to have higher motives. And perhaps the constant pursuit of honour and of the esteem of men, may produce an undue elation of mind unfriendly, and unsuitable to that humility, and that sense of our dependence and demerit, which religion requires.

To conclude, since we neither live, nor does it seem to be the design of providence that we shall ever live, in a utopian society, but among men surrounded with temptations, and whose interests interfere and cross on another in innumerable instances let us not expect perfection, in individuals, in societies, or in governments. We are conscious of many imperfections in ourselves.

Those who hold the reins of government are men of like passions, and have greater temptations.

*

The relation between a government and its subjects, like that of marriage, or of parent and child, is strong and important. It is a relation instituted by the author of nature, as without government, men must be savages. To preserve and strengthen this sacred tie, concerns the honour and the interest of both parties. The duties are reciprocal. Protection and the benefit of laws on one hand; respect, submission, and defense in time of danger on the other. Whatever is excellent in the constitution, ought to be the boast and the glory of the subject, as we glory in the virtues of our near relations. If we see, or think we see, imperfections in the constitution or in the government, we ought to consider that there never was a perfect human government on earth; We ought to view such defects, not with a censorious and malignant eye, but with that candor and indulgence with which we perceive the defects of our dearest friends. It is only atrocious conduct that can dissolve the sacred tie. While that is not the case, every prudent and gentle mean should be used to strengthen and confirm it. As is a good friend or neighbour with whom we can live in peace, amity and the exchange of good offices; so it is a good government under which we can lead quiet and peaceable lives in all godliness and honesty.

Bibliography

Ferguson, Adam. *An Essay on the History of Social Society*, Edinburgh, 1776.
— *Lectures on Pneumatology and Moral Philosophy, author's original manuscript*, Edinburgh University Library, EUL Dc.1.84-86.
— Yasuo Amoh (ed.), *The Papers of Adam Ferguson*, Edinburgh University Library, Rinsensha, 1996.
Gerard, Alexander. *Lectures of Alexander Gerard, taken by Robert Morgan, Aberdeen University, Mareshall College 1758-9* EUL D.C.8.18.
Hume, David. *Treatise of Human Nature : being an attempt to introduce the experimental method of reasoning into moral subjects*, London, 1793.
— *Three Essays, Moral and Political*, Edinburgh, 1748.
— *Political Discourses*, Edinburgh, 1752.
MacLaurin, Colin. *An Account of Sir Isaac Newton's Philosophical Discoveries*, London, 1748.
Ogilevie ,William. *An Essay on the right of Property in Land, with respect to its foundation in the law of nature: its present establishment by the municipal laws of Europe; and the regulations by which it might be rendered more beneficial to the lower ranks of mankind*, London, 1781.
Reid, Thomas. Knud Haakonsen (ed.), *Practical Ethics*, Princeton University Press, Princeton, 1990.
— Paul Wood (ed.), *Thomas Reid on the Animate Creation*, Edinburgh University Press, Edinburgh, 1995.
— Paul Wood (ed.), *The Correspondence of Thomas Reid*, Edinburgh University Press, Edinburgh, 2002.
Smith, Adam. *The Theory of Moral Sentiments*, London, 1759.
— The Wealth of Nations, London, 1776.
— *Essays on philosophical subjects by the late Adam Smith ; to which is prefixed, an account of the life and writings of the author by Dugald Stewart*, London, 1795.
— *Lectures on Jurisprudence*, Oxford University Press, Oxford, 1978.
— *Lectures in Rhetoric and Belles Lettres*, Oxford University Press, Oxford, 1983.

Steuart, James. *An Inquiry into the Principles of Political Economy*, London, 1767.

Stewart, Dugald. "Account of the life and Writings of Thomas Reid, D.D.F.R.S. Edinburgh, late Professor of Moral Philosophy in the university of Glasgow, Read at different meetings of the Royal Society of Edinburgh, Edinburgh and London, 1803, in Thomas Reid", William Hamilton(ed.), *The Works of Thomas Reid Vol.1*, James Thin, Edinburgh, 1895.

Wallace, Robert. *Various Prospects of Mankind, Nature and Providence*, London, 1761. (For his biography, B.Barnett Cochran, *Oxford Dictionary of National Biography*, Oxford University Press, Oxford et al., 2004).

Index

Aristotle, 140
Army, 18, 33, 34, 38, 48, 79, 80, 93, 122, 124, 126, 175
Astronomy, 10, 11, 21-23, 25, 26, 42, 45, 60

Benevolence, 44, 57

Cicero, 25, 140
Civil, society, 13, 42, 111, 117
Civilized, society, 41, 55
Commerce, 40, 47-49, 50, 54, 59, 66-69, 71, 73-80, 88, 108, 112-114, 126, 127, 172
Commonwealth, 108, 117, 133, 148, 153, 158, 192
Constitution, 34, 36, 37, 42, 117, 119, 125, 134, 135, 137, 141-150, 152-155, 160, 168, 181, 182, 200
Corruption, 9, 12, 44, 48, 49, 117, 119, 144, 153, 155, 157, 183
Credit, 76, 86, 90, 91, 128, 194

Demosthenes, 124, 140

Election, 33-35, 180
Empire, 2, 3, 8, 11, 33, 69, 73, 118, 121, 124, 150
Emulation, 20, 23, 145, 146, 156, 192
Enthusiasm, 43, 140, 142, 144, 164
Experiment, 5, 6, 11, 14, 19, 67, 73, 123, 142, 156, 157

Freedom, 37, 40, 87, 88, 116, 117, 126, 164, 167, 172
Frugality, frugal, 83, 194

Harrington, James, 133, 140
Humanity, 44-47, 50, 165

Improvement, 17, 22, 45, 49, 69, 70-72, 75, 91, 102, 103, 109, 113, 117, 119, 127, 138, 139, 162, 167, 168, 174, 176, 177, 179, 182, 183, 196, 198
Kingdom, 33, 37, 43, 46, 49, 101, 115, 128, 151, 155

Landed, property, 17, 174, 175, 178, 196
Legislator, 161
Liberal, art, 45, 60, 171
Liberty, 9, 10, 14, 15, 30, 31, 34, 35, 37, 47-50, 63, 74, 76, 85, 86, 88, 89, 91, 118, 119, 145, 150-152, 160, 182
Locke, John, 5, 7, 166
Luxury, 3, 4, 8, 16, 43, 44, 48-52, 54, 55, 79, 80, 96, 171, 187, 188, 192

Manufacture, manufacturer, 3, 47, 54-56, 59, 62, 64, 68, 69, 72-74, 76, 78, 95, 98, 99, 101, 103, 104, 108, 109, 110, 112, 113, 165, 171, 172, 177, 178
Mathematics, 60, 190
Mechanical, art, 45, 108, 109, 112
Mercantile, state, 123
Militia, 172
More, Thomas, 17, 20, 133, 137, 140, 141, 153, 160, 185, 193

Natural, law, 17, 167
Natural, philosophy, 10, 22, 42
Natural, price, 6, 59, 61-64, 75
Natural, right, 164-167, 172
Natural, state, (state, of, nature), 76, 141, 157, 168, 183

Original, contract, 7, 8, 29, 30, 32, 33, 39, 42, 43, 141

Plato, 17, 43, 133, 140
Politeia, 17, 53
Political, right, 126, 164
Political, spirit, 117, 124

Population, 8, 13, 15, 16, 23, 37, 86, 100, 103, 126, 178
Private
  interest, 85, 92, 93, 142, 184, 189, 191, 193, 195, 196
  property, 2, 14, 15, 41, 42, 69, 137, 141, 185-192, 195, 198
Prosperity, 10, 90, 101, 164, 166, 167, 171, 172, 182
Prudence, 57, 83, 195
Public, spirit, 13, 48, 50, 92-94, 120, 144, 189

Reason, 109, 152, 183
Refinement, 43-50, 69, 77, 87, 91, 112, 113, 116, 117, 121, 126, 167, 171
Republic, republican, republicanism, 7, 13, 14, 33, 34, 38, 48, 116, 118, 119, 123, 124
Revolution, 7, 8, 15, 16, 19, 22, 34, 36, 42, 47, 88, 91, 101, 102, 105, 140, 142, 144, 152, 154, 182

Slave, slavery, 49, 50, 70, 73, 74, 87, 91, 115, 139, 147, 150, 194
Stability, 3, 4, 8, 10, 37, 181, 190
Standing, army, 79, 80
Statesman, 13, 84, 87, 88, 92-94, 96-106, 110, 120, 124

Utopia, 16-20, 51, 133, 137, 145, 146, 148-150, 152, 153, 154, 156, 159, 160, 185, 186, 188-199

Virtue, 8, 11, 14, 19, 25, 41, 43, 48-52, 75, 77, 78, 90, 117, 118, 119, 120, 135, 145, 148, 151, 152, 155, 160, 161, 164, 170, 172, 178, 183-185, 187-189, 192, 198-200
Vulgar, 47, 78, 116, 121, 147

War, 10, 31, 37, 39, 42, 46, 47, 48, 49, 69, 73, 79, 80, 90, 91, 108, 110, 114, 116, 120, 121-126, 129, 159, 160, 179, 194